McGraw-Hill's

500 SAT Critical Reading Questions

to know by test day

Also in McGraw-Hill's 500 Questions Series

McGraw-Hill's

500 SAT Critical Reading Questions

to know by test day

Monica P. Lugo

Mc Graw Hill Education

New York   Chicago   San Francisco   Athens   London   Madrid
Mexico City   Milan   New Delhi   Singapore   Sydney   Toronto

Monica P. Lugo is an editor with more than 10 years of experience in test preparation, career development, educational, and general reference publishing, working in a wide range of formats, from trade paperbacks to online resources.

1 2 3 4 5 6 7 8 9 10 11 12 13 14 15 16 17   QFR/QFR   1 0 9 8 7 6 5 4 3

ISBN   978-0-07-182060-8
MHID   0-07-182060-4

e-ISBN   978-0-07-182059-2
e-MHID   0-07-182059-0

Library of Congress Control Number 2013936205

SAT is a registered trademark of the College Entrance Examination Board, which was not involved in the production of, and does not endorse, this product.

McGraw-Hill Education products are available at special quantity discounts to use as premiums and sales promotions or for use in corporate training programs. To contact a representative, please visit the Contact Us pages at www.mhprofessional.com.

This book is printed on acid-free paper.

CONTENTS

INTRODUCTION

Congratulations! You've taken a big step toward SAT success by purchasing *McGraw-Hill's 500 SAT Critical Reading Questions to Know by Test Day*. We are here to help you take the next step and score high on your SAT exam so you can get into the college or university of your choice!

This book gives you 500 SAT-style multiple-choice questions that cover all the most essential reading material. The questions will give you valuable independent practice to supplement your regular textbook and the ground you have already covered in your English and reading classes. Each question is clearly explained in the answer key.

The majority of critical reading questions on the SAT follow either a single reading passage or a pair of passages that are connected in some way. These questions are designed to determine how well you understand the information presented in the passage or passages. More than two-thirds of this book is devoted to items presented in this format. However, there are also critical reading questions that feature sentence completion. The later chapters of this book cover this question type.

This book and the others in the series were written by expert teachers who know the SAT inside and out and can identify crucial information as well as the kinds of questions that are most likely to appear on the exam.

You might be the kind of student who needs to study extra a few weeks before the exam for a final review. Or you might be the kind of student who puts off preparing until the last minute before the exam. No matter what your preparation style, you will benefit from reviewing these 500 questions, which closely parallel the content, format, and degree of difficulty of the critical reading questions on the actual SAT exam. These questions and the explanations in the answer key are the ideal last-minute study tool for those final weeks before the test.

If you practice with all the questions and answers in this book, we are certain you will build the skills and confidence needed to excel on the SAT. Good luck!

—*Editors of McGraw-Hill Education*

SAT Reading Comprehension

CHAPTER 1

Set 1 Questions

More than 150 years passed from the signing of the Declaration of Independence to the establishment of the national archives. As a result, priceless information was lost. Many documents were stolen or destroyed.

For example, a fire in 1921 consumed the records of the census taken in 1890. This census had differed from previous ones. For the first time, each   5 family received its own record. It contained expanded inquiries on race, home ownership, the ability to speak English, immigration, and naturalization. It also included a question relating to Civil War service.

Had these records survived, we would have inimitable information on these issues, as well as American industrialization, westward migration,   10 veteran services, and other characteristics of the American population at that time.

The data would have been incredibly enlightening and useful in limitless applications—to historians, political scientists, and so on—but it is now completely lost to history.   15

It is really quite remarkable that so many valuable records even exist today. Unfortunately, it wasn't until the twentieth century that the government became vigilant and proactive about the safety and preservation of historical records.

1. As used in line 4, the word "consumed" most nearly means
   (A) obsessive
   (B) devoted
   (C) extreme
   (D) incinerated
   (E) devoured

2. The author describes the records of the 1890 census as "inimitable" (line 9) because

   (A) the format was modeled on the censuses being used in Europe
   (B) they would have given us unique, reliable insights into nineteenth-century American life
   (C) there are no other records of who served in the Civil War
   (D) we could have used them to formulate current immigration law
   (E) they are the only U.S. census records with information about Abraham Lincoln's family

3. Based on the passage, all of the following are true about the 1890 census EXCEPT

   (A) It contained detailed questions.
   (B) Individual families obtained their own records.
   (C) It was used to learn about Civil War veterans.
   (D) It was unlike prior ones.
   (E) It was printed in a number of languages.

4. As used in line 18, the word "vigilant" most nearly means

   (A) protracted
   (B) mawkish
   (C) superficial
   (D) attentive
   (E) obsequious

5. Which of the following statements best supports the author's conclusion?

   (A) It is time-consuming to wade through historical records.
   (B) The 1890 census was the first to use punch cards.
   (C) America's historical records were completely ignored in the twentieth century.
   (D) A large number of census schedules are incomplete.
   (E) A special building where archives could be properly stored was built in 1930.

The human body creates a lot of heat. In addition to that which we create by running or jumping, we constantly use energy on involuntary functions such as blinking or blood circulation. These types of processes must go on at all times in the body, without our control, even during sleep. But unlike reptiles, which use only outside sources to heat and cool their bodies, mammals maintain a consistent temperature. Therefore, heat must be controlled, be the source from the outside environment or from our own bodily functions. 5

The body disperses heat into the air by exhaling warm, humidified air and by evaporating sweat. The evaporation of sweat cools both the skin and the blood in the vessels beneath it. This blood then returns to your core, cooling your internal 10 body temperature.

These processes work best when the ambient temperature is around 70 degrees. It begins to become less efficient when the temperature starts to match our core body temperature of 98 degrees. It also does not work as well when the humidity in the air rises, since the rate of evaporation slows down. That's when you begin to 15 feel hot and uncomfortable.

6. All of the following statements can be inferred from the passage EXCEPT

   (A) To reduce energy costs, air-conditioning systems should be turned on only when the room's temperature rises above 70 degrees.
   (B) Heat is a by-product of work being done by the body.
   (C) Because of the nature of our body's temperature control mechanism, we need a cooler ambient temperature for it to function optimally.
   (D) Humidity has a significant effect because it interferes with the evaporation of sweat.
   (E) Humans living in cooler climates have less efficient body temperature controls than those who live in warmer climates.

7. Based on the information in lines 2–4, another example of an "involuntary function" performed by the human body could include

   (A) chewing
   (B) walking
   (C) breathing
   (D) sniffing
   (E) eating

8. The author mentions reptiles in lines 4–5 in order to

(A) explain the difference between reptiles and insects

(B) suggest that humans and reptiles share many evolutionary traits

(C) emphasize the importance of temperature regulation for all living things

(D) provide a comparison with the way that mammals deal with temperature changes

(E) imply that reptilian temperature regulation is superior to that of humans

9. The "core" described in line 10 is most analogous to the body's

(A) system

(B) center

(C) extremities

(D) origins

(E) molecules

10. As used in line 12, the word "ambient" most nearly means

(A) stoic

(B) botanical

(C) surrounding

(D) fictitious

(E) punctilious

Food production takes an enormous toll on our environment. There are many procedures involved in the manufacture of food that result in greenhouse gases and other pollutants entering the environment. Some procedures require the consumption of copious amounts of fossil fuels, such as the transportation and refrigeration of food products. The trucks, trains, and planes that carry food around the world 5 are fueled by hundreds of thousands of gallons of gasoline. The electricity required to keep food refrigerated and preserved for human consumption requires the burning of coal or natural gas at power plants. Other factors that detrimentally affect the environment include excessive use of fresh water for irrigation.

The production of beef is more damaging to the environment than that of any 10 other food we consume. Grazing is a primary concern. Raising large numbers of cattle requires the production of a vast amount of food for the animals. It is estimated that producing one pound of beef requires about seven pounds of feed. Therefore, with the increase in the number of cattle farms comes ever-increasing demand for plant-based food production, which has its own, though less intense, 15 environmental impact. It also means grain crops that could be used for human consumption or for renewable energy such as biofuels must be used to feed the cattle.

Land use is also a problem. If the cattle are free-range cattle, large areas of land are required for them to live on. In some developing countries, this has led to dev- 20 astating deforestation and, subsequently, the loss of rare plants and animal species, particularly in tropical rain forests in Central and South America.

Another problem specific to beef production is methane emissions. Some microbes in the stomachs of cattle carry out a process known as methanogenesis, which produces methane. Methane's effect on global warming correlates with 25 changes in methane content in the atmosphere. While many people are aware of the damaging effects of carbon dioxide, they do not realize that methane's global warming potential is 25 times worse, making it a more dire concern.

Unfortunately, beef consumption is growing rapidly. This is the result of simple supply and demand factors. Specifically, there are two main causes of demand that 30 are spurring the production of more supply. First, the increase in the world population that has taken place since the advent of modern medicine means that there are more people to consume meat. The second factor is socioeconomic advancement. As citizens in developing nations become financially stable, they can afford to buy more meat. 35

Therefore, the only way to reduce the greenhouse gas emissions is for people around the world to significantly cut down on the amount of beef they eat.

11. The author's primary purpose is to
   (A) condemn the practice of deforestation of the rain forest
   (B) explain the effects of the population explosion beginning in the twentieth century
   (C) describe the history of global warming activism
   (D) argue for the reduction of pollution through a decrease in beef production
   (E) introduce legislation for a maximum portion of beef served in restaurants

12. The conclusion above is flawed because
   (A) governments, companies, and individuals are already doing a lot to reduce the carbon footprint of the beef industry
   (B) it doesn't take into account other methods of reducing greenhouse gas emissions
   (C) the beef diet for the average American adult each year is 150 pounds
   (D) cutting down on beef consumption would directly increase malnutrition in developed nations
   (E) raising animals doesn't require the additional, unique considerations that plant production does, such as fertilizer, insecticides, and irrigation

13. As used in line 4, the word "copious" most nearly means
   (A) prosaic
   (B) profuse
   (C) dubious
   (D) amicable
   (E) impeccable

14. According to the passage, which of the following statements can be inferred about beef production?
   I. The practice of raising free-range cattle is friendlier to the environment than traditional methods.
   II. Beef production generates a lot of greenhouse gases because the cattle release large amounts of methane.
   III. The money to be made by raising cattle is a motivating factor in cutting down otherwise unprofitable rain forests.
   (A) I
   (B) II
   (C) I and II
   (D) I and III
   (E) II and III

15. The author would most likely agree with which of the following statements?
    (A) Beef production generates more greenhouse gases than production of any other food we consume.
    (B) Developing nations consume too much of the world's beef.
    (C) Food production is a more dire concern than global warming.
    (D) The scientific community needs to find a way to stop methanogenesis in cows' stomachs.
    (E) Global warming is the direct result of advances in modern medicine.

16. As used in line 8, the word "detrimentally" most nearly means
    (A) obsequiously
    (B) destructively
    (C) informatively
    (D) cooperatively
    (E) sanctimoniously

17. Lines 16–18 suggest that the author regards biofuels as
    (A) a better alternative to natural gas
    (B) having a difficult time gaining public acceptance
    (C) a boon for the economies of nations in Central and South America
    (D) the unfortunate result of a growing world population
    (E) a more important use for grain crops than feeding livestock

18. As used in line 28, the word "dire" most nearly means
    (A) mundane
    (B) urgent
    (C) fortuitous
    (D) garrulous
    (E) deliberate

19. The primary purpose of the fifth paragraph (lines 29–35) is to
    (A) emphasize the socioeconomic advantages of beef production
    (B) explain the growing scale of the beef production industry
    (C) delineate the global warming issues that plague our society
    (D) illustrate the effect of modern medicine on the beef industry
    (E) criticize the unhealthy diet of developed nations

20. As used in line 25, the word "correlates" most nearly means

(A) rejects
(B) gesticulates
(C) corresponds
(D) deciphers
(E) obfuscates

21. In lines 33–35, the author implies that along with financial success comes

(A) sociopolitical conflict
(B) a more robust daily diet
(C) an understanding of supply and demand factors
(D) more use of modern medical techniques
(E) an increase in nationalized citizenship

22. According to the passage, methane is a serious environmental concern because

(A) the process of methanogenesis is deadly to humans
(B) the cattle can become sick from overabundant emissions
(C) its potential effect on the environment is many times greater than that of carbon dioxide
(D) most people are unaware of the existence of methane as part of the atmosphere
(E) it forms a toxic gas when it is combined with carbon dioxide

23. As used in line 28, the word "potential" most nearly means

(A) hegemony
(B) umbrage
(C) iniquity
(D) capability
(E) qualm

Passage 1

It is well known and documented that pregnancy in women over 40 brings an increased probability of health complications for the baby. For example, a woman's risk of having a baby with chromosomal abnormalities increases with her age. The most well-known complication of advanced maternal age is Down syndrome, a genetic disorder where the baby presents with both cognitive problems and physi- 5
cal irregularities.

What is not commonly known is that recent studies have revealed that men over 40 also risk passing on serious medical conditions to their children. In addition to problems such as low birth weight, advanced paternal age can cause schizo-
phrenia, bipolar disorder, and autism. Scientists are focusing their research on 10
sperm—mainly its genetic quality, but also its volume and mobility, all of which typically decrease with age—as a possible cause.

Passage 2

The cerebral cortex is the outside part of the brain that looks like a maze. Much like the intestines, the shape allows for more surface area in a confined space. The cerebral cortex plays a fundamental role in memory, attention, perceptual aware- 15
ness, thought, language, and consciousness.

Studies have found that in people with brain disorders that originate during fetal development, such as autism, certain areas of the cerebral cortex are shaped differently than those of healthy people.

Therefore, there must be a link between problems in the physical development 20
of the brain during pregnancy and mental illnesses.

24. Which one of the following statements can be inferred from Passage 1?

   (A) Medical, intelligence, and psychiatric screening should be mandatory for all parents.
   (B) Until recently, the role of older fathers in health problems was not public knowledge or fully investigated by scientists.
   (C) Too much sperm creates problems for the children of older fathers.
   (D) The number of older fathers has decreased in the past couple of decades.
   (E) More research could lead to better therapies or cures for these mental illnesses.

25. What topic do Passages 1 and 2 have in common?

   (A) The shape of the cerebral cortex
   (B) New treatments and therapies for autism patients
   (C) The risks of pregnancy in women over 40
   (D) Causes of health problems during pregnancy
   (E) Research into the paternal age effect

26. As used in line 5 of Passage 1, the word "presents" most nearly means
    (A) exhibits
    (B) emulates
    (C) vindicates
    (D) reproaches
    (E) quells

27. Which one of the following statements best supports the main point of Passage 2?
    (A) Dolphins, whales, apes, and even dogs have similar folds in their cortexes.
    (B) The size of a person's brain indicates certain personality traits and intellectual ability.
    (C) Disorders may be triggered when the nerves that pull the cortex into place are damaged during fetal development.
    (D) Parents can mold the size and shape of their child's brain after birth through vitamin supplements.
    (E) Phrenology has been increasingly accepted as more than just a pseudoscience.

28. The phrase "chromosomal abnormalities" in line 3 of Passage 1 refers to
    (A) mental illnesses
    (B) the cerebral cortex
    (C) physical deformities
    (D) genetic malformation
    (E) low birth weight

29. Which of the following, if true, would most undermine the assertion in the second sentence of Passage 1?
    (A) The reported link between autism and vaccines has been completely discredited.
    (B) Down syndrome is the most common chromosomal abnormality in humans.
    (C) Complications during the fetal stage are less likely to occur in teen pregnancies.
    (D) In a recent study, only 13 percent of people polled knew that Down syndrome is a health complication from pregnancy in women over 40.
    (E) Mothers from middle- and upper-class families are less likely to experience fetal health problems.

30. The author of Passage 2 mentions the intestines in order to

(A) illustrate the meandering nature of the brain's structure

(B) emphasize the size of the human appetite

(C) suggest a link between the brain and the digestive system

(D) imply that the brain is analogous to the stomach

(E) provide a contrast to the shape of the kidneys

31. In line 6 of Passage 1, the word "irregularities" most nearly means

(A) deviations

(B) rejuvenations

(C) avarices

(D) mercenaries

(E) prodigies

32. The major difference between the passages is that Passage 1 is concerned with

(A) pregnancy, while Passage 2 is concerned with fertility

(B) physical irregularities, while Passage 2 is concerned with mental illness

(C) Down syndrome, while Passage 2 is concerned with autism

(D) genetics, while Passage 2 is concerned with fetal development

(E) advanced maternal age, while Passage 2 is concerned with advanced paternal age

33. As used in line 15 of Passage 2, the word "fundamental" most nearly means

(A) intolerant

(B) disreputable

(C) essential

(D) generic

(E) tranquil

Charter schools are public schools—they receive public money, and they don't charge tuition, have a religious affiliation, or admit students through a selective admissions process. However, they are founded by entities such as nonprofit companies, individuals, universities, and state education boards, and are managed more like a private school.   5

A charter school is created by a contract—or charter—that outlines the school's mission and delineates a system for evaluating whether the school has met those goals and objectives, instead of having to adhere to state laws regulating school performance.

Charter schools are free from those regulations, and are held accountable for   10 academic results rather than the quotas that hamper success at other public schools. Thus, they are the best type of primary and secondary educational institution, and there should be more of them in every district in the United States.

34. Based on the last paragraph, the author would most likely describe nonchartered public schools as

(A) ineffective
(B) rebellious
(C) spasmodic
(D) odoriferous
(E) plebeian

35. In line 8, the word "adhere" most nearly means

(A) fasten
(B) exhort
(C) condescend
(D) insinuate
(E) obey

36. In the second paragraph (lines 6–9), the author suggests that

(A) public schools should have more regulation
(B) religion should be a part of public school education
(C) state laws restrict progress and achievement
(D) nonprofit companies have no place in primary and secondary education
(E) a selective admissions process is not important

37. It can be inferred from the passage that the author believes that
   (A) not every public school has the right mission
   (B) academic results are equal to success
   (C) public schools should be run by the federal government
   (D) more charter school students attend college
   (E) private schools are the best competition for charter schools

38. Which of the following most seriously undermines the author's conclusion?
   (A) Charter schools tend to be small, so they provide students with specialized attention.
   (B) Charter schools drain away funds that could be used for regular public schools.
   (C) Charter schools increase competition, enhancing the quality of all public schools.
   (D) Communities that are dissatisfied with nonchartered public schools are grateful for these alternative institutions.
   (E) Many charter schools have closed because of poor management or inferior academic performance.

39. The primary purpose of the passage is to
   (A) promote an increase in the number of charter schools
   (B) advocate for a decrease in funding for charter schools
   (C) explain the origins of charter schools
   (D) provide sample goals and objectives of certain charter schools
   (E) describe the most successful of all charter schools

With the world's population swelling and the water supply dwindling, the availability of fresh water for human consumption is a growing concern.

Conventional ways of getting more fresh water—such as using geological surveys to find new sources of fresh water underground or building dams in arid places such as Nevada to manage the flow of river water—are expensive endeavors. 5 These projects can double the cost per cubic meter for fresh water.

Steps have also been taken to encourage developed nations to use water more economically. Manufacturers now produce toilets that need almost no water to remove waste, as well as dishwashers that are much more efficient. Public awareness campaigns are also common, urging people to use less water during their daily 10 routine, such as when they shower or brush their teeth. While these steps are laudable, more needs to be done.

As sources of water disappear and the price gap closes, desalination of ocean water is growing in popularity. However, it is still a more costly and complicated way to get fresh water when compared with traditional methods. 15

40. As used in line 4, the word "arid" most nearly means
   (A) insatiable
   (B) scorched
   (C) deleterious
   (D) sedentary
   (E) ephemeral

41. Which of the following statements support(s) the main point of the passage?
   I. Less than half of one percent of human water needs is currently met by desalination.
   II. It can cost several dollars to produce a cubic meter of desalted water, while drawing fresh water from a river can cost as little as 10 cents.
   III. Desalination is the process of removing excess salt and other minerals from water.

   (A) I
   (B) II
   (C) III
   (D) I and II
   (E) II and III

42. Which of the following is NOT mentioned as a possible cause of decreased availability of fresh water?

    (A) An increasing world population
    (B) A smaller number of fresh water sources
    (C) The harmful effects of desalination to the environment
    (D) Wasteful use of fresh water in developed nations
    (E) The cost of establishing new fresh water projects

43. As used in line 12, the word "laudable" most nearly means

    (A) nonchalant
    (B) praiseworthy
    (C) resilient
    (D) acerbic
    (E) untoward

44. Lines 11–12 suggest that the author believes that

    (A) desalination is a problematic and unwise solution
    (B) dishwashers should be made much more efficient
    (C) geological surveys are the key to more fresh water sources being found
    (D) developed nations are still too careless with fresh water supplies
    (E) public awareness campaigns have been ineffective

"These benches were on the other side," Nana said quietly.

She stared around the room with eyes like saucers, looking long over every tile on the floor and in the wall. Papa wasn't too sure that she could handle walking up the famous Ellis Island staircase, but she was adamant. It was my first time in New York City. Nana had not been here in ages. 5

"How long were you in this room?" I asked. I was amazed that she had stood in this enormous entryway when she was my age. It seemed so long ago.

"It felt like hours and hours and hours, but I'm sure it was not that long. The inspector . . . he was Irish, too! He stood right there. He said he could tell mama was from County Cork. Then he marked her coat with chalk, and told her to fol- 10 low the group on the left, the one being sent to the hospital."

"She was sick? But she lived in New York for many years, you said!" I interjected.

On her face crept a small, mischievous smile. In a voice so low, as if she were afraid someone might overhear, she said, "No, no! Not sick. We were just too poor 15 to eat well on the ship. She had given me most of her food! She looked fragile, but she was tough as old boots. My Da, in his many letters, had warned her not to go to the hospital, no matter what. So she sat down on the bench, and as I stood, as she fussed with the collar of my dress, and she said very closely in my ear, 'Wipe the chalk with your elbow. Quickly!' How I trembled as I rubbed her coat! 20 'Quickly!' she said again. I got off as much of it as I could. Then we stood up and mixed in with a large group leaving out that door over there."

As her smile spread wide across her face, I laughed heartily. What a great story! But my father's look was serious and his eyes glistened in the bright sun that streamed into the hall through the enormous windows. "You never told me that 25 before, Mama," he said softly, tremulous. "So brave! You were both so very brave."

"No," said Nana, "we were scared and hungry, but we just knew we had to see Da again. He was waiting for us, with a job at the mill and a room to live in. We were sure that in America, there were better days to come."

45. As used in line 4, the word "adamant" most nearly means

    (A) resolute
    (B) bountiful
    (C) pretentious
    (D) conformist
    (E) penitential

46. In line 2, the phrase "with eyes like saucers" means that Nana was

    (A) wearing large, thick glasses
    (B) investigating for proof of alien life-forms
    (C) looking around in awe, with eyes wide open
    (D) too busy cleaning dishes
    (E) unable to stop crying

47. The narrator uses the repetition of the word "Quickly!" (line 21) mainly to
    (A) contrast with the way the inspector spoke to Nana
    (B) illustrate that Nana was too young to follow orders
    (C) criticize the inspector for putting the chalk on Nana's coat
    (D) emphasize how slowly Nana moved in her old age
    (E) indicate the fear and urgency that Nana's mother felt

48. The author uses the expression "she was tough as old boots" (line 17) to mean that Nana's mother was
    (A) stout but nimble
    (B) sick and tired
    (C) wise but scared
    (D) strong and brave
    (E) tall and skinny

49. The narrator would likely describe Nana's story about wiping the chalk from her mama's coat using which of the following terms?
    (A) thrilling
    (B) poignant
    (C) innocuous
    (D) emotional
    (E) nimble

50. As used in line 14, the word "mischievous" most nearly means
    (A) circuitous
    (B) translucent
    (C) contrite
    (D) playful
    (E) laborious

51. It can be inferred from the passage that Nana's father
    (A) abandoned Nana and her mother for another woman
    (B) was on his way to the American Southwest
    (C) had gone to America ahead of them to find work
    (D) believed that Nana and her mother had died en route to America
    (E) was waiting for them in County Cork, Ireland

52. As used in line 13, the word "interjected" most nearly means

(A) foreordained

(B) officiated

(C) interrupted

(D) desecrated

(E) rescinded

Passage 1

The Sumer was an extraordinary civilization in Mesopotamia (now southern Iraq) that lasted nearly 3,000 years. Historians believe that the Sumer civilization began possibly around 5,000 BC and was the first to practice full-scale agriculture, which gave rise to urban settlements. This is because the farming and cultivation created a surplus of storable food, so people no longer had to migrate.   5

As these remarkable people began to create permanent settlements, it initiated a need for the division of labor and the organization of the labor force. These advancements in human society created the need for recordkeeping, and thus they began to develop the written word around 3,500 BC.

Their exceptional achievements of agriculture, city settlements, and writing are   10 why the Sumer civilization deserves the title of "cradle of civilization" for all of humanity.

Passage 2

The history of wine is intriguing, but remarkably unclear. We do not have indisputable proof of where wine was first created.

Evidence of early winemaking has been found from North Africa to South   15 Asia. It is plausible that early foragers made alcoholic beverages from wild fruits, including grapes. That means that people may have been making wine for more than 10,000 years. Experts believe that they discovered that fermented fruit beverages were safe to drink by accident, after attempts to store fruit for later consumption were unsuccessful.   20

So while we have evidence of the consumption of wild fruits as part of the human diet, we cannot prove definitively where and when they were used to make wine. Early humans would have likely created small rations of wine, for consumption by family members only. The earliest evidence we have of full-scale agriculture sites that focused on wine production dates to 4,500 BC.   25

We also cannot gather archaeological evidence of winemaking before the use of pottery as a storage vessel for wine, which did not take place until around 6,000 BC. After the pottery is dated to a specific time period, we can then look for the organic compounds that are commonly found in wine. For now, using current scientific methods, there is simply no way to know exactly where and when wine   30 was first made.

53. According to lines 2–3 in Passage 1, the Sumer civilization was the first

(A) to practice full-scale agriculture
(B) group of people to set foot in Mesopotamia
(C) to outlaw migration
(D) to invade urban settlements
(E) civilization to cook food

54. In lines 4–5 of Passage 1, the author states that the people of the Sumer civilization no longer needed to migrate because they

    (A) moved from Mesopotamia to southern Iraq

    (B) developed the written word

    (C) created a surplus of storable food

    (D) had an organized labor force

    (E) no longer needed recordkeeping

55. It can be inferred from Passage 2 that

    (A) large-scale production of wine must have been in the region where wild grapes were first domesticated

    (B) evidence of wine has only been conclusive when taken from hard, nonwooden vessels with porous surfaces

    (C) wine production didn't take root in Europe until the Greeks began producing it around 4,500 BC

    (D) the ancient Chinese made wine from native wild grapes until they imported European grape seeds in the second century

    (E) while pottery was used as far back as 25,000 BC, the earliest known use of pottery as a vessel for food was around 10,500 BC

56. The authors of both passages discuss

    (A) differences in regional wine production

    (B) the development of language

    (C) the first use of pottery as a storage vessel

    (D) the early stages of full-scale agriculture

    (E) the beginnings of the written word

57. All of the following are reasons given in Passage 1 for the development of the written word EXCEPT

    (A) creation of permanent settlements

    (B) the need for the division of labor

    (C) migration away from Mesopotamia

    (D) the need for recordkeeping

    (E) organization of the labor force

58. Which of the following is a primary difference between passages 1 and 2?

   (A) The dates regarding the Sumer civilization in Passage 1 are more specific than the dates regarding the earliest wine production in Passage 2.

   (B) Passage 1 is more speculative about early human behavior than Passage 2.

   (C) Agriculture is the focus of Passage 1 but is largely ignored in the discussion about winemaking in Passage 2.

   (D) Passage 2 discusses the advantages of staying in one place more than Passage 1 does.

   (E) Sumer is inferred to be one of the earliest wine producers in Passage 1, while Passage 2 states this directly.

59. As used in line 14 of Passage 2, the word "indisputable" most nearly means

   (A) pugnacious

   (B) litigious

   (C) palatial

   (D) subservient

   (E) irrefutable

60. In the last paragraph of Passage 1, the author expresses

   (A) disdain for permanent urban settlements

   (B) confusion over the need for recordkeeping in ancient societies

   (C) admiration for the accomplishments of the Sumerians

   (D) disappointment in the writings of Mesopotamian cultures

   (E) support for modern labor unions

61. In Passage 2, the author mentions "current scientific methods" (lines 29–30) in order to

   (A) emphasize the scale of early winemaking vineyards

   (B) provide a timeline that illustrates just how old the practice of winemaking is

   (C) imply that current archaeological evidence is invalid

   (D) commemorate the achievements of early scientific investigations

   (E) suggest that with more advanced technology, we may be able to prove wine's origins

62. Compared to the tone of Passage 2, the tone of Passage 1 is more

    (A) laudatory
    (B) frustrated
    (C) apathetic
    (D) patronizing
    (E) compassionate

63. The conclusion of Passage 1 is most weakened by all of the following statements EXCEPT

    (A) Large, complex cities in India date as far back as 3,300 BC.
    (B) Writing developed in China around 4,000 BC and in Mesoamerica around 900 BC.
    (C) The Olmec of south-central Mexico laid the foundation for the Mesoamerican civilizations that followed it.
    (D) Agriculture allowed people to be artisans and priests instead of just hunters.
    (E) The Xia Dynasty in China had sophisticated urban settlements and bronze tools dating to 2,100 BC.

64. According to Passage 2, winemaking began as a result of

    (A) trade between Europe and the spice islands of Asia
    (B) trial and error with early attempts at food storage
    (C) the practices of early medicine men
    (D) scavenging the forests for food left by animals
    (E) children being left in charge of storage containers

65. As used in line 10 of Passage 1, the word "exceptional" most nearly means

    (A) deliberate
    (B) incomparable
    (C) harrowing
    (D) saccharine
    (E) hackneyed

The current energy crisis over crude oil threatens the political and social stability of all countries, regardless of their economic development. First, it creates increased political tensions between nation-states. Ever-increasing demand—especially from developing nations such as India, Brazil, and China—will eventually outstrip global supply. Estimates of how much crude oil there is vary, but what is 5 certain is that there is a finite amount of crude oil on the planet and, eventually, the supply will run out. As supplies diminish, this will lead to conflict, and possibly even war, between the nations that supply the crude oil and those that require the product.

Second, the energy crisis serves to further marginalize the poor, who will find 10 themselves priced out of transportation options, and maybe even food. As the standard of living improves in countries like India, Indonesia, China, and Brazil, more people move to big cities, where the jobs are, or they travel there from their homes in nearby towns. With more employment, they are then able to save money to purchase automobiles and the gasoline to fuel them. However, high-priced 15 gasoline means that they lose access to the educational and job opportunities that were previously available to them. The few public transportation options that exist are poorly maintained, further inhibiting their progress. Even in developed nations, costly gasoline has a profoundly detrimental effect on underprivileged communities. 20

Food availability is a problem, because logistics are dependent on crude oil. The food that is grown or produced must be transported from its point of origin out to markets around the world. The more expensive gasoline is, the more costly the food will be, since producers will need to increase the price of the final product in order to cover their cost of operations. Even staples like bread, milk, and rice 25 will become more expensive, threatening the ability of the world's poor to put food on the table.

Although crude oil is crucial to daily life, few nations today have access to large, easily recoverable deposits. Those that do, such as Venezuela and Iran, are currently involved in tense political and ideological disagreements with most other 30 nations in the developed world. Therefore, in order to avoid dependence on hostile nations, the oil and gas industries in countries like Canada and the United States have turned to unconventional methods of extracting crude oil from less accessible areas, such as tar sands and shale rock deposits.

These methods, while necessary, are nascent and controversial. For example, 35 some experts believe that more studies need to be done on the effects of the hydro-fracking process to remove oil and natural gas from shale rock. While some studies conclude that the process is safe for the environment, other studies show that it causes earthquakes and pollutes local water supplies. And in some cases, unconventional methods of oil and gas extraction are prohibitively expensive. 40

As a result of these issues, many national governments and major oil companies are working on developing other sources of energy, such as solar panels, wind farms, hydroelectric plants, and fuel from corn. However, many of these methods are still in their infancy. The technology has not evolved to the point where the

energy derived is dependable. For example, low rainfall means that the output 45
from hydroelectric plants drops precipitously. Power utilities still need plants that
run on fossil fuels to make up the shortfall. Another renewable option is nuclear
power. Although it has been in use by some countries for several decades, many
nations feel that the risks are too great. A nuclear meltdown would be unpredictable, deadly, and catastrophic—be it caused by a natural disaster or human 50
failure.

For now, the world economy depends on the production and dissemination of
crude oil. Therefore, with global demand for oil accelerating, the best way to avoid
dangerous conflicts is to get more fuel-efficient cars on the roads, to reduce our
dependence on driving by offering incentives for walking and bicycling, and to 55
build more effective public transportation systems.

66. Based on the passage, the author would most likely describe the current
energy crisis as

(A) the cause of underfunded hydrofracking studies
(B) a dangerous and urgent threat to global peace and economic stability
(C) a consequence of ambitious automobile marketing campaigns
(D) the reason why food production has not met the demands of
a growing world population
(E) the impetus for research into sources of water pollution

67. As used in line 35, the word "nascent" most nearly means

(A) omniscient
(B) zealous
(C) burgeoning
(D) pernicious
(E) inherent

68. In the fourth paragraph (lines 28–34), the author suggests that

(A) unconventional methods of extracting crude oil are impossible
(B) tar sands or shale rock deposits are found only in North America
(C) Venezuela and Iran are dependent on oil from hostile nations
(D) political tensions are shaping the progress of the oil industry
(E) easily recoverable deposits can be found all over the world

69. Which of the following statements best describes the "problem" mentioned in the third paragraph (lines 21–27)?
    (A) The production of crude oil is dependent on logistics and food availability.
    (B) The high cost of gasoline means the poor lose access to educational and job opportunities.
    (C) The cost of operations for food producers depends on the ability of workers to find adequate transportation options.
    (D) Locally grown food is a healthier and more cost-effective option for the poor.
    (E) Producers will raise prices, which means the poor will be unable to purchase sufficient amounts of even the most basic food products.

70. As used in line 46, the word "precipitously" most nearly means
    (A) scurrilously
    (B) demurely
    (C) vacuously
    (D) sharply
    (E) languidly

71. Which of the following most accurately describes the purpose of the sixth paragraph (lines 41–51)?
    (A) To highlight the effect of low rainfall on the environment
    (B) To describe the problems surrounding the development of alternative sources of energy
    (C) To explain how renewable sources currently have the largest share of the energy market
    (D) To illustrate the harmful effects of the hydrofracking process
    (E) To rebut the assertion that power utilities are too dependent on fossil fuels

72. As used in line 33, the word "unconventional" most nearly means
    (A) tacit
    (B) alternative
    (C) maudlin
    (D) delectable
    (E) concomitant

73. Which of the following statements is NOT supported by the passage?

    (A) The energy derived from renewable sources is not dependable.
    (B) The crude-oil supply quandary threatens the political and social stability of all countries.
    (C) Substantial, easily recoverable deposits are no longer common.
    (D) More public transportation options need to be available around the world.
    (E) Hydrofracking allows for the extraction of infinite deposits of crude oil.

74. As used in line 52, the word "dissemination" most nearly means

    (A) juxtaposition
    (B) suspension
    (C) locomotion
    (D) distribution
    (E) protrusion

75. Line 35 suggests that the author regards unconventional methods of extracting crude oil as

    (A) new technologies that are essential, but experimental and divisive
    (B) the only method available to meet the considerable current global demand for energy
    (C) an inexpensive way to put an end to the energy crisis
    (D) incompatible with other sources of energy, such as wind or solar power
    (E) available only in areas that have renewable energy options as well

76. Which of the following statements would reconcile the discrepancy in the last paragraph?

    (A) The current energy crisis will most likely worsen before it gets better.
    (B) Other forms of energy consumption, such as electricity for homes and businesses, are not a significant factor in the current energy crisis.
    (C) Governments around the world have not enacted any laws or policies to curb dependence on individual car ownership.
    (D) Higher prices at the gas pump would go much further in convincing people to drive less.
    (E) Crude oil production around the world, but especially in the Middle East, has stagnated since the 1970s.

77. The reason why some nations do not use nuclear power (lines 48–51) is that

    (A) the cost of running nuclear power plants is too high
    (B) there is no longer a need for nuclear energy
    (C) the effect of a plant meltdown would be too devastating
    (D) the energy produced is too short-lived
    (E) it violates their ideological beliefs

78. As used in line 50, the word "catastrophic" most nearly means

    (A) calamitous
    (B) violent
    (C) cogent
    (D) innocuous
    (E) momentary

The books of Jane Austen often emphasize the fact that women lacked economic stability and social protections in the eighteenth and nineteenth centuries in Europe. Their fates were inextricably linked to the men in their lives. Women could not inherit property. If a woman was not fortunate enough to be born into a prosperous family, she had few options. Women who were not from middle-class or upper-class families were unlikely to receive much education. Most women were not trained in specific professions. The most common jobs included working in a factory, or as a teacher, a maid, or a governess. The only recourse was to find a husband.

In addition to her keen observations on society at large, Jane Austen likely drew on her own experiences with education and marriage in European society as she crafted her famous novels. While Austen grew up in an openly scholarly home, where her writing was encouraged, she was aware that this was not the norm. Her family was not affluent, as her father could not support his family solely on his salary as a pastor and often supplemented his income by farming and teaching. She, her mother, and her sister frequently depended on the kindness of family members upon his death. Regarding marriage, the only proposal Austen ever received, and did not accept, was from a friend who was well-to-do, but whom she did not love.

Thus, many Austen characters, such as Fanny Price in *Mansfield Park* and Charlotte Lucas in *Pride and Prejudice*, are women who are educated but have little money, and therefore must consider marriage to men they do not care for in order to have financial security. In addition, Austen's first published novel, *Sense and Sensibility*, begins with the death of Mr. Dashwood. His estate passes to his only son from a first marriage, so Mr. Dashwood's second wife and his daughters have no legal claim to stay in their own home.

79. Which of the following statements best describes the main point of the passage?

(A) Austen's only sister, who was also unmarried, was her closest friend.
(B) Austen's heroines are some of the most beloved in English literature.
(C) The role of women in society is a frequent subject in Austen's novels.
(D) Austen was bitter and depressed, because she could not marry due to her lack of income.
(E) According to Austen, the events in the novel *Sense and Sensibility* were autobiographical.

80. The author provides examples of various Austen heroines in order to

(A) illustrate Austen as a master of literary realism
(B) compare them to the heroines of female novelist George Eliot
(C) critique the sentimental novels of the late eighteenth century
(D) support the theory of recurring themes in Austen's novels
(E) foreshadow the failure of Austen's publishing career

81. As used in line 3, the word "inextricably" most nearly means

(A) audaciously
(B) extravagantly
(C) thoroughly
(D) convulsively
(E) pretentiously

82. Based on the passage, the author would most likely describe the lives of women in the eighteenth and nineteenth centuries as

(A) spontaneous
(B) expeditious
(C) penitential
(D) precarious
(E) ambidextrous

83. Which of the following statements is supported by the passage?

(A) Even with an education, it was difficult for women to earn a living of their own.
(B) Marriages between people of different economic classes were rare.
(C) Austen was never able to depend on her family for assistance.
(D) Women in the eighteenth and nineteenth centuries could work only in the home.
(E) Austen resented her father for his choice of profession.

84. As used in line 8, the word "recourse" most nearly means

(A) censure
(B) option
(C) jargon
(D) anecdote
(E) bulwark

Passage 1

The South Bronx has experienced a significant urban renewal and is nearly unrecognizable from the nadir seen in the 1970s. This renewal is evident, starting with rehabilitated and new residential structures, including multifamily town homes, apartment buildings, and prefabricated ranch-style homes. Much of the new development has taken place in vacant lots in traditionally poor areas.　　5

Popular commercial restaurants and retail chains, such as Applebee's, Marshalls, Staples, and Target, have opened stores, which have turned many formally dismal areas into desirable places to live.

Other efforts to improve traditionally poor neighborhoods are underway, such as petitions for granting landmark status to the Grand Concourse, in recognition　10 of the area's Art Deco architecture. The Yankees baseball franchise also recently razed "the house that Ruth built" and replaced it with a state-of-the-art stadium, which was completed in time for the start of the 2009 baseball season. Along with the new billion-dollar field, athletic fields, bicycle and walking paths, stores, restaurants, and a new Metro-North railroad station will be opened.　　15

The South Bronx is also home to both for-profit and nonprofit organizations that offer a range of professional training and other educational programs, as well as a renewed grassroots art scene. Clearly, the South Bronx is experiencing a much-deserved renaissance, both of the physical appearance of the borough and for its residents.　　20

Passage 2

Although there have been considerable improvements since the 1970s, the South Bronx is still a long way from sustained prosperity. It contains over half of the Bronx's housing projects, and nearly half of the people in the South Bronx eke out an existence below the poverty line.

Many of the problems that have plagued the area since the "Bronx is burning"　25 days, such as drug trafficking, gang activity, and prostitution, are still common. In fact, the South Bronx still has some of the highest violent crime rates in all of New York City.

Certainly, there are pockets of progress. The South Bronx has experienced substantial new building construction and renovations in the 2000s, and national　30 retailers have begun to open stores in the borough, attracting new business and residents.

Nevertheless, this is largely true of areas within or around the outskirts of traditionally stable, affluent areas of the Bronx, such as the city blocks directly surrounding Yankee Stadium, as well as the Riverdale neighborhood, which is far　35 away in the northwest part of the borough. The fact is, most of the areas that fell into terrible decay in the late twentieth century remain lost in an endless spiral of poverty.

85. Which one of the following statements most accurately expresses the main idea of Passage 1?

(A) The South Bronx is home to numerous for-profit and nonprofit organizations.

(B) The Grand Concourse should be granted landmark status.

(C) A socioeconomic revitalization is taking place in the South Bronx.

(D) The Yankees baseball franchise is the savior of the South Bronx.

(E) Manhattan residents flock to the South Bronx for its renewed grassroots art scene.

86. As used in line 8 of Passage 1, the word "dismal" most nearly means

(A) miserable

(B) seditious

(C) exemplary

(D) blithe

(E) vociferous

87. Which of the following statements most accurately describes the relationship between Passage 1 and Passage 2?

(A) Passage 1 is a direct rebuttal of the ideas in Passage 2.

(B) Both passages arrive at the same conclusion through different analyses.

(C) Passage 1 provides an alternative theory to that of Passage 2.

(D) The passages address the same topic but arrive at different conclusions.

(E) Passage 2 provides the evidence to support the conclusions in Passage 1.

88. Compared with the author of Passage 1, the author of Passage 2 displays an attitude that is

(A) pessimistic

(B) supercilious

(C) appreciative

(D) flippant

(E) mendacious

89. As used in lines 23–24 of Passage 2, the phrase "eke out" most nearly means to

    (A) infinitely vex
    (B) paralyze outright
    (C) completely abstain
    (D) wholly consecrate
    (E) scrounge together

90. In the final sentence of Passage 2, the author expresses

    (A) an optimistic appraisal of the South Bronx's entrepreneurial spirit
    (B) an affectionate ode to his hometown
    (C) a mixed evaluation of the mayor's efforts to revitalize the South Bronx
    (D) a cautious judgment of the effect of retail culture on the South Bronx
    (E) a cynical assessment of the South Bronx's current economic standing

91. As used in line 21 of Passage 2, the word "considerable" most nearly means

    (A) hedonistic
    (B) significant
    (C) prominent
    (D) absurd
    (E) inevitable

92. As used in line 12 of Passage 1, "the house that Ruth built" represents

    (A) the original stadium where Babe Ruth played
    (B) the mansion that the Yankees owner bought for Babe Ruth
    (C) the 161st Street subway station next to Yankee Stadium
    (D) the bullpen in the new Yankee Stadium, named after Babe Ruth
    (E) the childhood home of Babe Ruth

93. As used in line 12 of Passage 1, the word "razed" most nearly means

    (A) legislated
    (B) defiled
    (C) curtailed
    (D) demolished
    (E) suppressed

94. The authors of the two passages disagree on the topic of
    (A) how much the quality of life in the South Bronx has improved since the 1970s
    (B) whether the state government has done enough for the South Bronx
    (C) whether the burgeoning arts and music scene can outshine that of Manhattan
    (D) how little most people know about the role of the South Bronx in U.S. history
    (E) whether the residents of the South Bronx are happy with the Yankees' new stadium

95. It can be inferred from the passages that both authors would agree that the South Bronx
    (A) has been essentially ignored by the residents of the other boroughs
    (B) fell into deep disrepair in the late twentieth century
    (C) is congested with traffic because of the new Yankee Stadium
    (D) has lost its character due to the increase in national retail stores
    (E) has not seen any new construction over the last fifteen years

With advances in modern medicine, as well as more research and a more sophisticated understanding of chemistry, scientists are learning more about the effects of hormones on the human fetus.

Recent studies show that prenatal testosterone levels can affect many characteristics of physical abilities and attributes, as much as or even more than inherited 5
genetic factors.

The study found that testosterone levels can influence a man's athleticism, musical ability, facial symmetry, and even dancing ability.

Men who were exposed to higher prenatal testosterone levels tend to be better dancers, because they are more coordinated and better able to execute complex 10
choreography.

96. Which of the following statements can be inferred from the passage?
   (A) Men are more likely to be better singers than women.
   (B) Testosterone levels in the womb can increase a man's abilities in math and science.
   (C) Men who cannot dance well always have more trouble finding a mate.
   (D) The development of dancing in early human societies was merely a physical expression of a genetic trait.
   (E) Men exposed to more testosterone in the womb are more likely to have greater control over their bodies.

97. As used in line 1, the word "advances" most nearly means
   (A) improvements
   (B) omniscience
   (C) iniquities
   (D) suspensions
   (E) hostilities

98. According to the second paragraph (lines 4–6), higher prenatal testosterone levels could have a greater influence on a person's physical characteristics than
   (A) athleticism
   (B) inherited genetic factors
   (C) facial symmetry
   (D) knowledge of science
   (E) mental abilities

99. According to the passage, the reason why we know more about the human fetus today is because of

   (A) more studies on the effects of testosterone in women
   (B) progress in the field of chemistry and modern medicine
   (C) specific studies on testosterone in dancers
   (D) more prenatal doctor visits for young mothers
   (E) advanced studies on human DNA

100. As used in line 10, the word "execute" most nearly means

   (A) perform
   (B) attract
   (C) assassinate
   (D) venerate
   (E) rebuke

CHAPTER 2

Set 2 Questions

Common law systems, such as the one used in the United States, are based on court decisions from individual cases. That is, if a similar dispute has been resolved in the past, the court must adhere to the reasoning from the prior decision. Therefore, court decisions are considered to be binding laws.   5

Civil law systems, on the other hand, consist of a code of principles. Instead of following precedent, civil law systems emphasize jurisprudence, or the theory of law, and an understanding of legal reasoning.

Clearly, the civil law system is superior. The common law system's reliance entirely on prior decisions—also known as the principle of *stare deci-*   10
sis—means that its decisions can quickly grow outdated, and unfortunately, changing the law through the legislative process is slow and cumbersome.

101. Which of the following statements would most weaken the conclusion of the passage?

(A) Common law was developed in England and is found throughout the United Kingdom's former colonies.

(B) Since the United States is considered to be a free, just nation, the common law system is better than other legal systems.

(C) Basic laws regarding property or contracts cannot be created through legislation.

(D) The courts can revise laws without going through the legislative process on a few select occasions.

(E) Because of constitutional law, statutory law, and regulatory law, the U.S. legal system is too complex.

102. As used in line 7, the word "precedent" most nearly means

(A) previous example

(B) unlikely witnesses

(C) untoward advance

(D) lucky happenstance

(E) irrefutable proof

103. The author's attitude toward common law in the last paragraph indicates that the author

(A) sees common law as a stagnant, obsolete legal system
(B) feels that the United States should revise its constitution
(C) has the utmost respect for the legislative process
(D) wants to make Latin mandatory in U.S. schools
(E) rejects the civil law system because it originated in ancient Rome

104. According to the passage, the Latin words *stare decisis*

(A) are italicized because they are spelled incorrectly
(B) are a term for the guiding tenet of common law
(C) suggest that the civil law system is superior
(D) are unable to be translated into English
(E) delineate the process of legislation

105. As used in line 12, the word "cumbersome" most nearly means

(A) verdant
(B) unwieldy
(C) assiduous
(D) meager
(E) rancorous

The relentless rise of the Internet creates phenomena—from e-mail and instant messaging to social networking and file-sharing programs—that are transforming society. A new discipline, Web science, aims to discover how websites and customs arise and how they can be harnessed to benefit everyone. It involves observation of the micro interactions of people on the Web, such as instant-messaging conversa- 5 tions, as well as the macro effects of the Internet on the world stage, such as You-Tube stardom.

It also investigates the ways in which the dark side of the Internet's capabilities, such as identity theft and cyberstalking, can be anticipated and prevented. Web science studies are showing that the best way to prevent problems is to make Web 10 pages and Web interactions more trustworthy.

Best practices based on recent findings include visiting pages created by sources such as universities, as well as those that encourage the use of reputable services such as PayPal.

106. Which of the following statements best supports the author's main point?

(A) Intellectual property and copyright law for digital content is beginning to be expanded.

(B) Social norms have the greatest impact on the Web.

(C) Researchers found that the most useful and prolific sites provide dependable layers of security.

(D) The Web was originally created as a tool for researchers.

(E) The most relevant Web pages have the largest number of pages linking to them.

107. As used in line 4, the word "harnessed" most nearly means

(A) beleaguered

(B) rebuilt

(C) disposed

(D) bound

(E) utilized

108. As used in line 8, the phrase "the dark side" is symbolic of the

(A) destructive aspects of Internet use

(B) increased influence of the Internet

(C) legal ramifications of Internet use

(D) rapid proliferation of Internet use

(E) elegant language of the Internet

109. According to lines 3–4, Web science aims to

   (A) ascertain how Internet culture begins and how it can be used to help society
   (B) arrest the perpetrators of cyber crimes
   (C) deconstruct the origins of the computer
   (D) manage the costs of website development
   (E) educate the public on the dangers of websites

110. The author mentions "identity theft and cyberstalking" as

   (A) suggestions for improvements to Internet use
   (B) paragons of the best parts of the Internet
   (C) punishment to perpetrators of Internet crimes
   (D) examples of dangerous online activities
   (E) models of early Internet programs

111. The author uses "micro" and "macro" examples of Internet use to

   (A) propose a new online tool
   (B) emphasize the distance between Internet users
   (C) provide the scope of Web science's objectives
   (D) explain the size of a computer chip
   (E) imply that space and time are infinite

112. In the context of this passage, the word "interactions" most nearly means

   (A) consequences
   (B) exchanges
   (C) minions
   (D) platitudes
   (E) maelstroms

One day this summer, the groom cleaned and dressed me with such extraordinary care that I thought some new change must be at hand; he trimmed my fetlocks and legs, passed the tarbrush over my hoofs, and even parted my forelock. I think the harness had an extra polish. Willie seemed half anxious, half merry, as he got into the chaise with his grandfather. 5

"If the ladies take to him," said the old gentleman, "they'll be suited, and he'll be suited: we can but try."

At the distance of a mile or two from the village, we came to a pretty, low house, with a lawn and shrubbery at the front, and a drive up to the door. Willie rang the bell and asked if Miss Blomefield or Miss Ellen was at home. 10

In about ten minutes he returned, followed by three ladies; one tall, pale lady wrapped in a white shawl, leaned on a much younger lady, with dark eyes and a merry face; the other, a very stately-looking person, was Miss Blomefield. They all came and looked at me and asked questions.

"If you incline, you can have him on trial, and then your coachman will see 15 what he thinks of him," said Mr. Thoroughgood.

"You have always been such a good adviser to us about our horses," said the stately lady, "that your recommendation would go a long way with me, and if my sister Lavinia sees no objection, we will accept your offer of a trial, with thanks."

In the morning, a smart-looking young man came for me. I was led home, 20 placed in a comfortable stable, fed, and left to myself.

The next day, when my groom was cleaning my face, he said, "That is just like the star that Black Beauty had; he is much the same height too; I wonder where he is now."

A little further on, he came to the place in my neck where I was bled, and 25 where a little knot was left in the skin. He almost started, and began to look me over carefully, talking to himself.

"White star in the forehead, one white foot on the off side, this little knot just in that place. . . . It must be Black Beauty! Why, Beauty! Beauty! Do you know me? Little Joe Green!" 30

And he began patting and patting me as if he was quite overjoyed. I could not say that I remembered him, for now he was a fine-grown young fellow, with black whiskers and a man's voice, but I was sure he knew me, and that he was Joe Green, and I was very glad. I put my nose up to him, and tried to say that we were friends. I never saw a man so pleased. 35

"Give you a fair trial! I should think so indeed! You must have been badly served out somewhere. Well, well, it won't be my fault if you haven't good times of it now."

In the afternoon, I was put into a low Park chair and brought to the door. Miss Ellen was going to try me, and Green went with her. I soon found that she was a 40 good driver, and she seemed pleased with my paces. I heard Joe telling her about me, and that he was sure I was Squire Gordon's old Black Beauty.

113. It can be inferred from the passage that the narrator is a

(A) squire
(B) horse
(C) jockey
(D) soldier
(E) house

114. In the first paragraph, the narrator believes that "some new change must be at hand" (line 2) because he is

(A) given a delicious meal
(B) moved to a new stable
(C) greeted by new people
(D) being specially groomed
(E) taken to the veterinarian

115. The narrator describes Willie as "half anxious, half merry," meaning that Willie is

(A) weary, but hopeful
(B) jubilant, but kind
(C) nervous, but enthusiastic
(D) wary, but angry
(E) testy, but willing

116. Based on the context of the passage, a "chaise" is

(A) a new hairstyle
(B) a quilted seat cover
(C) a type of horse-drawn carriage
(D) a horse's groomsman
(E) the French word for "grandson"

117. As used in line 9, the word "shrubbery" most nearly means

(A) a brush
(B) signposts
(C) a barn
(D) bushes
(E) a sponge

118. Mr. Thoroughgood is offering Black Beauty to the sisters "on trial," meaning that

(A) they can observe whether he is a good fit without obligation
(B) they have to return him after thirty days
(C) the sisters have broken the law and need a lawyer
(D) they can only use him to pull their carriage on Sundays
(E) the horse was smuggled into the country illegally

119. As used in line 18, the word "stately" most nearly means

(A) frivolous
(B) dignified
(C) auriferous
(D) corpulent
(E) atrocious

120. When the stately lady says to Mr. Thoroughgood that "your recommendation would go a long way with me," she means that

(A) he has to travel far to reach her
(B) they will soon go on a journey
(C) communication is important to her sister
(D) it will be a long time before they speak again
(E) his advice is valuable to her

121. As used in line 19, the word "objection" most nearly means

(A) compromise
(B) protestation
(C) malediction
(D) subsistence
(E) reverence

122. The description of the tall lady in lines 11–12 suggests that she is

(A) wealthy
(B) annoyed
(C) frail
(D) buoyant
(E) ashamed

123. When the narrator says he was "placed in a comfortable stable" (line 21), he means that he

(A) became the property of Mr. Thoroughgood
(B) was left in a well-kept barn
(C) was taken to the racetrack
(D) was driven around town in a truck
(E) had unwavering faith in the sisters

124. It can be inferred that when the narrator says that Joe, the groom, "almost started" (line 26), he means that Joe

(A) nearly began to run
(B) was greatly surprised
(C) fell on his knees in a faint
(D) felt great pride in his work
(E) experienced a sense of fear

125. Based on lines 32–33, it can be inferred that the narrator doesn't remember Joe Green, because

(A) the narrator has been mistakenly drugged
(B) Joe has had plastic surgery
(C) Joe has grown up since the narrator last saw him
(D) the narrator is too old and senile
(E) the narrator lost his eyesight in an accident

126. When Joe says that the narrator was "badly served out" (lines 36–37), he means that the narrator was

(A) given bad-tasting food
(B) in a great line of work
(C) mistreated
(D) promoted at work
(E) taken in from the cold

The moon is thought to have formed more than four billion years ago, not long after Earth. There have been a number of hypotheses on how it came to exist, but the most widely accepted explanation is that an impact occurred between Earth and another object that was likely as big as Mars, which forced tons of material into orbit. All that material then coalesced to form the moon. It is now in synchro- 5
nous rotation, meaning the same side of the moon always faces Earth.

However, the far side of the moon may have faced Earth at one time. We know from the age of the craters on the moon's surface that it was hit repeatedly during the creation of the solar system. If the moon had always faced the same way, it would have more craters on one side. Therefore, an event—perhaps a collision 10
with a large asteroid—must have spun the moon 180 degrees to its current orientation.

127. It can be inferred from the passage that the author believes that

- (A) the formation of the moon does not coincide with the formation of the asteroid belt
- (B) there are several possible causes for there being just one moon orbiting Earth
- (C) there is an even number of craters on both sides of the moon
- (D) the age of the craters on the moon cannot be accurately determined with today's technology
- (E) there are aliens living on the far side of the moon

128. As used in line 5, the word "coalesced" most nearly means

- (A) ostracized
- (B) combined
- (C) vegetated
- (D) deteriorated
- (E) interrogated

129. In lines 2–3, the author suggests that

- (A) other explanations for the moon's existence have been deemed unlikely
- (B) there is no explanation for the moon's existence
- (C) people have ignored the moon's existence for thousands of years
- (D) people have been frightened by the moon for millennia
- (E) we will never know why the moon exists

130. In lines 3–5, the author implies that

(A) the moon was once in orbit around Mars

(B) Earth was once a gas giant like Jupiter or Saturn

(C) it is impossible for planets to collide with other planets

(D) the collision between Earth and the other object was colossal

(E) there is still a ton of material in orbit above Earth from that impact

131. The purpose of the text in lines 10–12 is to

(A) suggest a possible explanation for the moon's current orientation

(B) emphasize the size of the moon's craters

(C) provide a new hypothesis for the creation of the moon

(D) explain the names of the moon's craters

(E) imply that the moon is in danger of colliding with another celestial body

132. As used in line 12, the word "orientation" most nearly means

(A) sexuality

(B) zeitgeist

(C) position

(D) topography

(E) detriment

Peanut allergies are on the rise in the United States. Nearly one in 200 people has an allergy to peanuts. Many restaurant meals and prepackaged foods contain whole peanuts or peanut products, such as peanut butter or peanut oil. Allergic reactions are therefore difficult to avert for people who suffer from this allergy.

Children with this allergy are often at serious risk when eating foods outside   5
the home, away from the watchful eyes of their parents and guardians.

Many schools are adopting no-tolerance policies for peanuts on school premises. It is the only effective approach to protecting children who are allergic from suffering a fatal reaction.

133. The statistic provided in lines 1–2 serves primarily to

    (A) justify the no-tolerance policies adopted by many schools

    (B) prove the lack of sufficient numbers of nurses in public schools

    (C) compare the contents of peanut butter and peanut oil

    (D) present the number of peanut allergy–related hospital visits that take place every day

    (E) illustrate how common peanut allergies are in the United States

134. Which of the following statements undermines the conclusion stated in the last sentence?

    (A) Studies have found that the longer parents avoid introducing peanut products into their child's diet, the greater the risk of the child's developing peanut allergies.

    (B) Having epinephrine injectors in schools and alerting teachers about which children are afflicted keep incidents of reactions low.

    (C) Peanut allergy is distinct from nut allergies, such as those caused by almonds and walnuts.

    (D) Since deaths due to peanut allergies are relatively rare, the peanut allergy threat has been significantly inflated by the media.

    (E) The exact reason why a person develops a peanut allergy is unknown.

135. As used in line 4, the word "avert" most nearly means

    (A) assess

    (B) cajole

    (C) avoid

    (D) purloin

    (E) lacerate

136. According to the second paragraph (lines 5–6), children are most at risk when eating out because

(A) unstable people will try to poison their food with toxins
(B) they are unable to read food labels to learn the ingredients
(C) restaurants are not allowed to serve minors
(D) they are not being supervised by an adult who is familiar with their allergy
(E) they are less exposed to peanut products

137. A no-tolerance policy means that peanuts and peanut products

(A) are not allowed on school grounds
(B) cannot be removed from school grounds
(C) must be present at all times on school grounds
(D) have been seen on school grounds
(E) will soon be brought onto school grounds

The Inca civilization, which began in present-day Peru, set in motion an extensive expansion and conquest in the early fifteenth century of the tribes that lived in the Andean region.

There were many languages spoken by different tribes of peoples in the Andean region. The Incas took on one of the many dialects of Quechua that existed at the 5 time as their official language and imposed its use on the peoples that they conquered in order to ease communications across the empire, which stretched along nearly the entire western coast of the South American continent.

Many people mistakenly believe that Quechua was the native language of the Incas, because it is still spoken by their descendants. It is only because the Incas 10 went on to enlarge their empire in the 1400s through invasion and subjugation that Quechua became the *lingua franca* of the region. The Inca Empire would have survived, and Quechua would have retained this status, had it not been for the Spanish conquest at the turn of the sixteenth century.

138. Which of the following statements most weakens the author's conclusion?

(A) The last emperors of the Inca Empire were Huascar and his half-brother, Atahualpa.

(B) The Inca Empire was already on the brink of collapse when the Spanish arrived.

(C) The descendants of the Aymara people, conquered by the Incas, live primarily in the Lake Titicaca basin.

(D) It is likely that the inhabitants of Machu Picchu were wiped out before the Spanish arrived.

(E) The Spanish often erected new settlements, including the great capitals of Quito and Cusco, on top of the great cities of the Inca Empire.

139. As used in lines 1–2, the word "extensive" most nearly means

(A) widespread

(B) vulgar

(C) acoustic

(D) rebellious

(E) contrite

140. Which of the following statements is supported by the passage?

(A) Cusco, the capital city of Peru, was the capital of the Inca Empire.

(B) The Spanish made it illegal to speak Quechua until the twentieth century.

(C) The Inca Empire, at its peak, was extensive.

(D) The Spanish were less skilled at navigation than the Portuguese.

(E) Many Quechua words made their way into colloquial Spanish in Andean countries.

141. As used in line 11, the word "subjugation" most nearly means

(A) pantomime

(B) suppression

(C) leniency

(D) lunacy

(E) turpitude

142. It can be inferred from the passage that *lingua franca* means a language

(A) used to make communication possible between people who don't share a language

(B) that is so complex it cannot be translated into other languages

(C) conceived by the Incas for use only by the emperor and only during ceremonies

(D) that was created in the fifteenth century in France for universal use

(E) a predecessor of the twentieth century's Esperanto language

Music piracy has been a colossal problem for the recording industry ever since a student at Northeastern University named Shawn Fanning launched his world-famous online music file-sharing program called Napster in June 1999. Essentially, it allowed people to exchange files between computers, thereby circumventing the need to go to a store and purchase an album or single recording.   5

The Recording Industry Association of America sued Napster in December 1999 to prevent the exchange of copyrighted music through the program. Soon after, big-name recording artists such as Metallica, Dr. Dre, and Madonna also filed lawsuits.

The lawsuits were the biggest mistake that the recording industry ever made, 10 since it created the publicity that made Napster a worldwide phenomenon, and despite the efforts of companies, artists, and governments, new file-sharing programs appear every day.

143. Which of the following statements is the assumption on which this passage depends?

(A) Napster was most popular with college students in the greater Boston area.

(B) Napster made it easier for people to download songs that were hard to find.

(C) Napster paved the way for similar decentralized file-sharing programs.

(D) Napster was a relatively unknown service before lawsuits were reported in the news.

(E) File-sharing programs are beneficial to musicians who are not signed to major labels.

144. As used in line 4, the word "circumventing" most nearly means

(A) masquerading

(B) doling

(C) avoiding

(D) inquiring

(E) inverting

145. It can be inferred from the passage that

(A) Napster users predominantly shared digital music files

(B) Napster became popular on the west coast after Fanning moved to Los Angeles

(C) the RIAA was unable to win the lawsuit due to negative public opinion

(D) people stopped using Napster when their favorite artists spoke out against it

(E) Northeastern University offered Fanning a job after Napster became a worldwide phenomenon

146. With which of the following statements would the author most likely agree?

    (A) File-sharing programs are prolific, despite efforts to stop illegal downloads.

    (B) The recording industry embraced online music downloads because of Napster.

    (C) File-sharing programs are most useful for getting older songs and bootleg recordings of concerts.

    (D) Metallica drummer Lars Ulrich was vilified for his campaign against Napster.

    (E) The original Napster program was eventually shut down.

147. The dates included by the narrator in the passage reveal

    (A) that file-sharing programs were only used by high school students

    (B) how frequently people used the file-sharing program

    (C) that file-sharing has been around for more than fifty years

    (D) how quickly the RIAA moved to sue Napster

    (E) that Fanning was just sixteen years old when he wrote the Napster program

Passage 1

One controversial interaction that the fashion industry has with the public is the issue of "plus size" fashion—from models to specialty boutiques—which has both its champions and detractors.

Advocates for plus-size fashion marketing say that it is a positive step for an industry that has been corrupted by a preference for models who sometimes do not 5 even weigh 100 pounds. So in a literal sense, fashion models have traditionally been nearly half the size of the average American woman. Supporters of plus-size fashion say that the fashion industry—and by extension, the media—bombards people with images of women that are unhealthy and not at all realistic. Therefore, plus-size clothes and models are a step in the right direction. 10

However, others say that the term "plus size" in the fashion industry is a misnomer. Many times, the plus-size model is only a size 6, and even the largest model in the industry is still only about a size 10. Yet the average American woman is a size 14. So while the efforts of a number of high-profile designers to include "larger" models and bigger sizes in their recent collections are commendable, it is 15 still not representative of reality.

All these opponents, however, are still missing the most important point— plus-size fashion marketing should not exist at all. The proliferation of plus-size fashion clothing, as well as plus-size women being championed as role models, will only result in the acceptance of obesity in our society. This is tremendously damag- 20 ing, since obesity rates in the United States are on a continuous upswing. The industry is responsible for how it markets products and images to society, and therefore should only show images of people who are fit and trim.

Passage 2

The specter of eating disorders in the fashion industry is an ever-present issue. Experts estimate that many models at top agencies are as much as 20% under- 25 weight. The World Health Organization considers a body mass index (BMI) value of 16 to be severe thinness, but many models are well below that figure. The pressure to remain this thin is why some models resort to anorexia and bulimia, and this pressure often trickles down to women at large because of images in the media.

It is not hard to see why these disorders are pernicious, and so often deadly. 30 Model Ana Carolina Reston had a BMI of only 13 and weighed just 88 pounds at the time of her death at age 21 in 2006. That same year, model Isabelle Caro slipped into a coma after starving herself down to just 55 pounds.

In response to calls for more proactive measures, officials at some leading mod- eling events have implemented guidelines to encourage healthy body weights, such 35 as not allowing models with a BMI lower than 18 to walk the runway.

Clearly, the question remains of whether modeling agencies and top design companies have the ethical responsibility to move away from the ultrathin appear- ance that characterizes the industry. However, it is not up to the industry to edit its message. It is up to the models' guardians to make sure they are eating properly, 40 and up to parents of young women to help them have a healthy body image.

148. As used in line 24 of Passage 2, the word "specter" most nearly means

(A) presence
(B) banshee
(C) opulence
(D) protrusion
(E) effrontery

149. The author's primary purpose in writing Passage 1 is to

(A) discuss opinions about plus-size fashion
(B) explain the history of fashion nomenclature
(C) reveal the reasons behind U.S. obesity rates
(D) describe the process of running fashion shows
(E) justify the existence of catwalk models

150. The authors of the two passages would most likely disagree on

(A) which BMI the World Health Organization should accept as healthy
(B) how common eating disorders are in the fashion industry
(C) whether the industry is responsible for how it markets products and images to society
(D) which designers should be allowed to place ads in magazines
(E) whether overweight people should be allowed to purchase designer clothes

151. As used in line 8 of Passage 1, the word "bombards" most nearly means

(A) overwhelms
(B) obfuscates
(C) compromises
(D) frolics
(E) convulses

152. The author's attitude toward plus-size marketing in Passage 1 can best be described as

(A) extravagant
(B) tranquil
(C) subservient
(D) antagonistic
(E) conditional

153. As used in line 30 of Passage 2, the word "pernicious" most nearly means

(A) bountiful

(B) destructive

(C) inexhaustible

(D) antediluvian

(E) implacable

154. With which of the following statements would the author of Passage 1 most likely agree?

(A) Today's most prolific designers are the best the industry has ever seen.

(B) The fashion industry should emphasize a trim, athletic figure as the ideal body type.

(C) Designers need to produce more products in American factories.

(D) Designer knockoffs are a serious problem for the fashion industry.

(E) Different races and ethnicities are not represented in fashion magazines.

155. As used in line 34 of Passage 2, the word "proactive" most nearly means

(A) inconceivable

(B) energetic

(C) capricious

(D) mendacious

(E) neglectful

156. Both passages mention the fact that the fashion industry

(A) has been avoiding the topic of eating disorders among runway models since the mid-1970s

(B) in the United States is responsible for the abundance of plus-size models in Europe

(C) needs to combat the problem of fashion counterfeiting by shutting down illegal factories in countries such as China and India

(D) has been accused of portraying women's bodies through the media in ways that are harmful and unreasonable

(E) has taken a number of steps to address inconsistencies in sizing for women, including changing to a measurement system, like men's clothing has

157. As used in line 12 of Passage 1, the word "misnomer" most nearly means

(A) an unsuitable term
(B) a terrible insult
(C) an obvious lie
(D) a term of endearment
(E) a shining recommendation

158. In lines 39–41 of Passage 2, the author suggests that

(A) agencies and designers should not be blamed for the eating behaviors of their models or of adolescents in society
(B) models with a BMI lower than 18 should no longer be allowed to walk any runways in European and Asian shows
(C) the parents of Ana Carolina Reston and Isabelle Caro should sue their respective agencies for wrongful death
(D) the BMI of many models in the fashion industry is well below the figure that the World Health Organization considers to be severe thinness
(E) eating disorders are not an issue that agencies and designers need to take seriously at the moment

According to a recent report, rates in the United States are diminishing for both the diagnoses of new cancers, also known as incidence, and the death rate for all cancers combined. This is true for both men and women, especially in the most frequent cancers among men (lung, colon, and prostate) and women (breast and colon). This is the first time that these rates have shown such a decline (in inci-   5
dence and death rate, as well as in men and women) in the 15 years that records have been kept. However, the report finds significant differences in lung cancer death rate trends by state, and even by regions within states.

Deviation in smoking pervasiveness is influenced by several factors, including public awareness of the harm of tobacco use, tolerance of tobacco use within the   10
community, local tobacco control activities, and local promotional activities by the tobacco industry. The states where lung cancer death rates for women are on the rise have higher percentages of adult female smokers, low taxes on tobacco products, and local economies that have been dependent on tobacco farming and production for generations. In contrast, California was the first state to implement a   15
statewide tobacco control program that includes high taxes and laws against smok-ing in public places, such as restaurants and city parks, to reduce exposure to sec-ondhand smoke. And it was the only state to show declines in both lung cancer incidence and deaths in women.

Men and women continue to have higher incidence and death rates in areas   20
where tobacco use is deeply rooted in daily life, says the director of the North American Association of Central Cancer Registries. The geographic disparity in smoking-related cancers is therefore due mostly to behaviors, not environmental factors such as exposure to pollutants or chemicals, she adds. The report also draws a comparison between lung and skin cancers, which are both firmly influenced by   25
behavior.

Other highly encouraging findings revealed by the report include decreases in incidence and death rates in nearly all racial and ethnic groups. Once again, states with targeted programs have better results.

All these achievements, however, must be seen as a starting point rather than   30
a destination. A dual effort—better application of existing knowledge, as well as ongoing research to improve prevention, early detection, and treatment—will be needed to augment this progress into the future.

159. It can be inferred from the passage that

(A) progress is being made against all cancers, in particular the most common types

(B) more needs to be done to lower the incidence and death rates from cancer in certain ethnic groups

(C) more women pay the price with many types of cancer than men

(D) death rates for all smoking-related cancers are on the rise for women

(E) most states have vigorous tobacco control programs

160. As used in line 1, the word "diminishing" most nearly means

(A) aspiring
(B) exasperating
(C) vindicating
(D) consigning
(E) shrinking

161. Which of the following statements does the passage support?

(A) Changes in incidence can be caused by changes in screening practices.
(B) The regional differences in lung cancer trends highlight the success of tobacco control programs.
(C) Smoking accounts for approximately 30 percent of all cancer deaths.
(D) The drop in death rates has been steeper for men.
(E) There is not a lot of variation in tobacco smoking patterns across the United States.

162. California's tobacco control program is mentioned as an example of how

(A) all states should adopt more strenuous excise taxes
(B) those policies fail to protect citizens from the dangers of lung cancer
(C) statewide programs are more effective than local programs
(D) such programs can have a positive effect on cancer rates
(E) those programs differ from programs of other states

163. As used in line 9, the word "pervasiveness" most nearly means

(A) corrosiveness
(B) ubiquity
(C) resilience
(D) opulence
(E) recalcitrance

164. The author would probably agree that

(A) behavior can influence a change in an individual's chances of getting certain cancers
(B) more should be done to shame the tobacco industry into eliminating its marketing and publicity programs
(C) there are substantial differences in smoking behaviors in younger versus older populations
(D) the report does not show a definitive decline in cancer incidence for both men and women
(E) there is a delay in an expected decrease in lung cancer deaths among women, as well as a slowing of the decrease in lung cancer deaths among men

165. The second paragraph (lines 9–19) mostly serves to

    (A) explain why different states and regions have different lung cancer death rates

    (B) applaud promotional activities by the tobacco industry

    (C) recommend new local tobacco control activities

    (D) dissuade women from working in restaurants and city parks

    (E) warn against tobacco farming and production

166. The primary purpose of the passage is to

    (A) reveal that science cannot detect differences between cancer cells

    (B) question the differences in cancer incidence and death rates between racial and ethnic groups

    (C) provide an update on cancer trends, specifically smoking-related lung cancer

    (D) discuss trends in cancer treatment options in the United States

    (E) offer examples of new cancer detection options

167. The conclusion in lines 30–31 implies which of the following statements?

    (A) Efforts in prevention, early detection, and treatment should be frequently assessed and enhanced.

    (B) Cancer death rates have been plummeting since the first report was released.

    (C) This is the first concurrent decline in cancer incidence for both men and women.

    (D) The drop in incidence is something the National Cancer Institute has been waiting to see for a long time.

    (E) Decreases in incidence and death rates are being seen across the board.

168. All of the following are supported by explicit statements in the passage EXCEPT

    (A) Underserved, low-income cancer patients must be served in the communities where they live.

    (B) We must accelerate and improve our efforts in reducing the burden of cancer in this country.

    (C) Tobacco control programs have a positive impact on the toll of tobacco use.

    (D) Lung cancer continues to rob many people of a long, healthy life because of tobacco use.

    (E) The drop in incidences and mortality is evidence of real gains in prevention, early detection, and treatment.

169. As used in line 15, the word "implement" most nearly means

(A) juxtapose
(B) lacerate
(C) purloin
(D) preoccupy
(E) apply

170. Which one of the following describes the purpose of the third paragraph (lines 20–26) of the passage?

(A) To demonstrate the need for more research as described in the first paragraph
(B) To offer expert testimony to support the claims in the second paragraph
(C) To provide contrast to the evidence in the second paragraph
(D) To refute the claims made by the authors of the report in the last paragraph
(E) To confirm the information supplied in the first paragraph

171. Which of the following could be another example of the "environmental factors" mentioned in line 24?

(A) Pollution from automobiles
(B) High-stress workplace
(C) Long travel hours
(D) Employment in hotels
(E) Wildlife preservation

172. As used in line 33, the word "augment" most nearly means to

(A) discredit
(B) converge
(C) advance
(D) wrangle
(E) entrench

A hoarder is someone who is unable or unwilling to throw items away, and the disposal of items causes them considerable anguish. When people hoard a massive amount of objects, it takes over the livable spaces of their home. As the collection grows, they are unable to do simple, quotidian activities such as cooking a meal or watching TV. Sometimes the hoarding is so severe that portions of their homes   5 become inaccessible.

But among the many problems that such behavior brings about, the most significant are the health risks. Once hallways and windows are blocked, hoarders are at risk of dying in a fire, since they no longer have a clear path of evacuation. Piles that are stacked up high can fall on top of the homeowner, or a person trying to   10 climb over a stack of objects can experience a fall. There is also the problem of poor sanitation. Areas where food cannot be properly cleaned begin to attract roaches and vermin, and bathrooms that are full of many possessions can no longer be washed and scoured.

Unfortunately, the severity of the problem can escalate for two reasons. One is   15 that since the behavior progresses behind closed doors, people can amass collections of objects for years before friends or family members become aware of the problem. A second reason is that hoarders often do not recognize that they have a problem, and will continue to live in denial until they get professional help.

When attempting to make a diagnosis, psychologists do not categorize hoard-   20 ing as a disorder in itself. Instead, it is often seen as a symptom of obsessive-compulsive disorder (OCD), depression, anxiety, or attention-deficit hyperactivity disorder. The mental health community has only recently begun an intensive study of hoarding, and more research is needed in order to understand its causes and find effective treatment.   25

173. With which of the following statements would the author most likely agree?

(A) The most significant problem caused by hoarding is the economic burden.

(B) Luckily, hoarded items cannot be stacked higher than a person's head.

(C) Food preparation becomes easier the longer a person is a hoarder.

(D) Hoarding is a debilitating behavioral condition.

(E) Psychologists do not believe that hoarding is a real problem.

174. Which of the following statements most supports the author's conclusion?

(A) Hoarding is more prevalent in older men.

(B) People who hoard usually do not have other obsessive-compulsive symptoms.

(C) Mental health professionals are not doing enough to make the public aware of hoarding.

(D) There appears to be a strong genetic component to hoarding.

(E) Hoarding is a relatively new syndrome for the mental health community.

175. As used in line 4, the word "quotidian" most nearly means

(A) commonplace

(B) abnormal

(C) piquant

(D) unbroken

(E) pyrrhic

176. The first paragraph mostly serves to

(A) warn the public about obsessive-compulsive disorder

(B) illustrate how infrequent hoarding is

(C) introduce the problem of hoarding

(D) explain the connection between hoarding and depression

(E) dissuade psychologists from working with hoarders

177. As used in line 15, the word "escalate" most nearly means

(A) exploit

(B) canoodle

(C) delineate

(D) burnish

(E) intensify

Passage 1

During World War II, sending and receiving codes required hours of encrypting and decrypting. The Japanese used their considerable skill as codebreakers to intercept many messages being sent by American forces in the Pacific.

In an effort to find quicker and more secure ways to send and receive communications, the United States enlisted Navajo Indians to relay critical information 5 between military units.

The Navajo language was chosen in part because of its complex grammatical structure and syntax. In addition, it was still an unwritten language at that time and was spoken only on the Navajo lands of the American Southwest. As a result, the use of the Navajo language as a code was a remarkable success. Crucial battles, 10 including the famous Battle of Iwo Jima, were successful because of the use of the Navajo code. And after the war, Japan's chief of intelligence admitted they were never able to break it.

It is estimated that more than 400 Navajos served in this program, which remained highly classified until 1968. The codetalkers returned home without 15 fanfare after the war and were sworn to secrecy about the code's existence. For decades, the American people had no idea that the U.S. triumph in the Pacific theater was partly due to these courageous men. Luckily, the exploits of these heroic soldiers are finally making their way into mainstream American history.

Passage 2

Thanks to recent Hollywood movies and TV documentaries, when you mention 20 codetalkers, most people today immediately think of the now-legendary bilingual Navajo soldiers recruited during World War II. But in fact, this type of codetalking did not begin in that war, and Navajo was not the first language used.

The original codetalkers were Choctaw Indians from southeastern Oklahoma, and it was their language that was first utilized near the end of World War I. It is 25 said that an American officer got the idea to use Choctaw while serving in France. Overhearing a couple of Choctaw Indians in his company speaking to each other in their native language, he supposed that it would likely make an unbreakable code that the U.S. Army could use to get information past the Germans. His hunch proved to be correct. Choctaw soldiers were soon placed in each company, 30 and Choctaw was spoken over radio waves.

Although the Navajo codetalkers are the most famous, Navajo was not even the only Native American language used during World War II. Choctaw was also used, in addition to other languages, such as Cherokee, Lakota Meskwaki, and Comanche. 35

Clearly, the brave Choctaw soldiers who served as codetalkers should receive equal commemoration in society today.

178. Which of the following statements can be inferred from Passage 1?

    (A) The lack of military terminology in the original Navajo vocabulary was an obstacle.
    (B) Maintaining secrecy is vital to the national security of every country, particularly in wartime.
    (C) It took many decades for the Navajo nation to rise above cultural oppression.
    (D) The Navajo language was successful, because few people in the world could understand it.
    (E) Native Americans had successfully sent secure messages in previous wars, such as World War I.

179. The main point of Passage 2 is that

    (A) although the Navajo soldiers are the most renowned, they were not the original codetalkers
    (B) the representations of Choctaw Indians in movies and on TV are inaccurate
    (C) the now-legendary Navajos recruited during World War II were not bilingual
    (D) the Cherokee, Lakota Meskwaki, and Comanche languages were better codes
    (E) the Choctaw language was actually well known in France

180. The author of Passage 1 mentions the admission by the Japanese chief of intelligence in order to

    (A) provide an example of the tensions between the Allied and Axis powers
    (B) highlight the friendship between the United States and Japan
    (C) imply that the Japanese may have been lying about not breaking the code
    (D) suggest that the United States is the world's biggest superpower
    (E) emphasize just how successful the use of Navajo was as a code

181. As used in line 30 of Passage 2, the word "hunch" most nearly means

    (A) aspersion
    (B) domesticity
    (C) intuition
    (D) meditation
    (E) remission

182. Which of the following statements most accurately describes the relationship between Passage 1 and Passage 2?

(A) Passage 1 is a direct rebuttal of the ideas in Passage 2.

(B) Both passages arrive at the same conclusion through different analyses.

(C) Passage 2 provides an alternative perspective to the topic introduced in Passage 1.

(D) The passages address similar aspects of the same topic but arrive at different conclusions.

(E) Passage 2 provides the evidence to support the conclusions in Passage 1.

183. As used in line 18 of Passage 1, the word "exploits" most nearly means

(A) unimpaired conditions

(B) agreeable odors

(C) causes of distress

(D) courageous acts

(E) harsh denunciations

184. Which of the following most accurately describes the purpose of lines 20–22 in Passage 2?

(A) To criticize the portrayal of Native Americans in Hollywood

(B) To explain the renown of Navajo codetalkers in society today

(C) To exemplify the bravery of the Choctaw soldiers

(D) To describe the landscape of the Navajo nation

(E) To justify the use of real languages as military code

185. The author of Passage 2 would most likely respond to the conclusion of Passage 1 by pointing out that

(A) during World War I, the Choctaw nation was a self-governed republic

(B) Native American languages were unwritten

(C) Choctaw soldiers still do not receive the same recognition as Navajo soldiers

(D) the Battle of Iwo Jima would have been lost without the use of the Navajo code

(E) the Choctaw War Memorial was not erected until 1995

186. As used in line 16 of Passage 1, the word "fanfare" most nearly means

    (A) camaraderie
    (B) celebration
    (C) pantomime
    (D) orthodoxy
    (E) turpitude

187. The author of Passage 2 implies in lines 29–31 that

    (A) although Choctaw was used openly, it was never deciphered by the Germans
    (B) the British used the Welsh language to send messages between military units
    (C) the Choctaw did not refer to themselves as codetalkers
    (D) the Choctaw soldiers in World War I never received a medal of honor
    (E) Choctaw codetalkers served primarily in the Marine Corps

188. It can be inferred from the passages that both authors would agree that

    (A) the Navajo word for "potato" was used to refer to a hand grenade
    (B) Navajo was spoken only on the Navajo lands of the American Southwest
    (C) the U.S. Army owes many victories to the Native American codetalkers
    (D) codetalkers memorized all the terms, because codebooks could not be taken into the field
    (E) informal, shortcut code words were essential to getting a quick response

189. With which of the following statements would the author of Passage 1 most likely agree?

    (A) The codetalkers used symbolism for military terms not used in Navajo, such as grenade.
    (B) The idea to use Navajo was discussed by generals during the Spanish-American War.
    (C) The Navajo nation has the largest population of Native Americans in the United States
    (D) Navajo codetalkers are overrated and should remain in obscurity.
    (E) Navajo was the most successful military code in modern history.

190. As used in line 27 of Passage 2, the word "company" refers to

    (A) a theater group
    (B) a ballet troupe
    (C) a military unit
    (D) concert musicians
    (E) house guests

For thousands of years, people have been passionate about learning more about the Red Planet. The oldest records we have date to 2,000 BC and were made in ancient Egypt. From then on, we know that Chinese, Babylonian, Greek, Indian, and Islamic astronomers all kept notes and descriptions about Mars.

However, before the first use of the telescope by Galileo Galilei in 1610, obser- 5
vations of Mars consisted only of comprehensive annotations of its position, size, and distance from Earth. Eventually, as telescopes improved, astronomers established the planet's orbit, rotation period, and axial tilt, and eventually they created detailed maps. Specific features on the planet's surface were revealed, including dark patches on its red surface, as well as the existence of polar ice caps. 10

Today, humanity's infinite curiosity about Mars has taken us to uncharted territory. A number of unmanned spacecraft known as "rovers" have landed on Mars in recent years. Because scientists are able to control the mechanized rovers from Earth, millions of miles away, the exploration potential is limitless. With the rovers' ability to take pictures and recover actual samples of soil and rock from the 15
planet's surface, humanity continues to make new discoveries about the fourth planet from the sun.

191. "The Red Planet" (line 2) is used as a metaphor for Mars because

    (A) it is best seen in the red deserts of the American Southwest
    (B) the surface of the planet is red
    (C) people go to war when they see Mars through a telescope
    (D) the position of Mars affects people's moods, mostly making them angry
    (E) the god that Mars is named after wore a red robe

192. The author's attitude toward Mars observation can best be described as

    (A) patronizing
    (B) unsympathetic
    (C) enthusiastic
    (D) annoyed
    (E) incensed

193. The author's primary purpose in writing the passage is to

    (A) criticize the landing of spacecraft on Mars
    (B) explain how the Red Planet got its name
    (C) commemorate the astronauts who have been to Mars
    (D) describe the history of Mars observation
    (E) defend Galileo's reputation

194. With which of the following statements would the author most likely agree?

(A) This millennium has ushered in a new chapter in Mars observation.
(B) The ancient Egyptians were the most skilled astronomers in antiquity.
(C) The use of the telescope to observe Mars was a disastrous mistake.
(D) The latest rover landing revealed that there is life on Mars.
(E) Taking samples from the Martian surface is dangerous.

195. The phrase "unmanned spacecraft" (line 12) is analogous to a

(A) computer
(B) robot
(C) notepad
(D) trolley
(E) word processor

196. As used in line 11, the word "uncharted" most nearly means

(A) transcendent
(B) moribund
(C) ashen
(D) unexplored
(E) ubiquitous

The Tower of London was constructed as part of the conquest of England by armies from lands in present-day France. Led by William the Conqueror, the Normans invaded and occupied England toward the end of the eleventh century. The Tower itself was built in 1078. At first, it was a residence for the royal family, and therefore became a symbol of the power and oppression inflicted upon the citizens 5 of Great Britain by these new rulers.

However, the Tower was later used for a number of other purposes, including as an armory, a treasury, and a public records office.

Today, it is most famous for having been a prison. Many notable figures were imprisoned there at one time, especially in the sixteenth and seventeenth centuries, 10 including Elizabeth I before she became queen, and her mother, Anne Boleyn, before she was executed. Despite its infamous reputation, however, executions at the Tower were extremely rare.

197. As used in line 5, the word "inflicted" most nearly means

(A) imposed
(B) abrogated
(C) rebuked
(D) deigned
(E) impinged

198. According to the passage, the Tower's use as a royal residence

(A) came to symbolize the tyranny of the Norman conquerors
(B) was unsustainable because it cost too much to maintain
(C) is the use that most people today think of when the Tower is mentioned
(D) only occurred during William the Conqueror's lifetime
(E) is evident from the majestic tower's architecture

199. As used in line 12, the word "infamous" most nearly means

(A) quixotic
(B) scurrilous
(C) nimble
(D) preoccupied
(E) notorious

200. The author mentions the rarity of executions at the Tower in order to

(A) provide proof that the Normans were not evil
(B) illustrate how much British culture has changed
(C) imply that executions are more frequent today
(D) suggest that executions in Great Britain should be legalized
(E) emphasize that the Tower's reputation is unfounded

CHAPTER 3

Set 3 Questions

A mysterious ailment called colony collapse disorder (CCD) has wiped out large numbers of honeybees. The exact cause of the problem is as yet unknown, but there are a number of theories. Many experts believe that the colonies may have been hit by viral or fungal infections. Other possible causes include malnutrition, poison by fertilizers and pesticides, and a loss 5 of genetic diversity as a result of commercial breeding. Recent studies have revealed that there is likely more than one factor affecting the bees, rather than a single cause.

The loss of these bees is both an environmental and economic disaster. They are responsible for the pollination of numerous plants in the wild, as 10 well as crops. This symbiotic relationship means that if the bees disappear permanently, so will the wild plants that depend on them to reproduce. The honeybees that are cultivated for commercial use are also affected by CCD. This means that many of the common foods that we consume regularly, including fruits and almonds, could become so rare that they will 15 become luxuries rather than diet staples. More research needs to be done to find the actual causes of CCD in order to remedy this dire situation.

201. With which of the following statements would the author most likely agree?

(A) Professional and amateur beekeepers are affected by CCD, as are stationary and migratory populations in the wild.

(B) Even before CCD, honeybees suffered from a number of ailments that affected the numbers in their populations.

(C) There are no patterns of loss in the affected populations.

(D) Researchers believe that there is a single cause of CCD, rather than several.

(E) Bee colonies affected by CCD have been found in South America and Central Asia.

202. All of the following are possible causes of CCD EXCEPT
    (A) The honeybees are being harmed by manmade substances, such as pesticides.
    (B) The colonies suffer from pathogens that are baffling researchers.
    (C) The pollination of luxury crops keeps bees from pollinating wild plants.
    (D) Commercial breeding may be causing reproductive problems and genetic mutations.
    (E) The honeybee's natural defenses may be lowered by poor nutrition.

203. Which of the following statements would most undermine the author's conclusion?
    (A) Federal and state governments are not taking proactive steps based on definitive findings on the causes of CCD.
    (B) Viral infections in insects are mostly found in U.S. midwestern states and in Europe.
    (C) Amateur beekeepers are better prepared for outbreaks of CCD than professionals at big companies.
    (D) Research into the causes of CCD is well funded by private investors.
    (E) As long as people keep consuming fruits and almonds, CCD will continue to plague honeybees.

204. It can be inferred from the first paragraph that
    (A) it is more important that we solve the economic consequences than that we worry about the environmental effects of CCD
    (B) CCD is caused by humans altering the environments they live in with flowers and plant species that are not indigenous
    (C) CCD could be cured if only there were more advances taking place in the creation of antiviral drugs
    (D) the causes of CCD are complex, which is why research has shown that one single trigger is not a likely scenario
    (E) only commonly consumed food crops are affected by CCD, not specialty foods

205. The "symbiotic relationship" of bees and plants (line 11) is analogous to

(A) elephants and antelopes that share the same watering hole during the hot summer months in Africa

(B) cleaner shrimp that feed off the bacteria living on bigger fish that would otherwise make the bigger fish sick

(C) tapeworms that enter the intestinal tracts of mammals and feed off the host until it dies

(D) the breeding of horses for use as part of various modes of transportation

(E) the larval stage of insects before metamorphosis into adulthood

There are several forms of age-related bias, or ageism. One of the most insidious is discrimination against the elderly. It often takes the form of older people being marginalized or patronized out of pity. People will often speak to the elderly in a slow, infantile manner, or they will assume that the senior citizen is a needy, nonproductive member of society.

This kind of discrimination is often described as "benevolent prejudice," because the interactions between people are often friendly. There are no outward signs of anger or fear. But in fact, the elderly are often seen as bungling and ineffectual, and are therefore treated differently, despite there being absolutely no proof of ineptitude. The term "benevolent prejudice" is also often used to describe the discrimination perpetrated against women and the disabled.

Ageism toward the elderly often manifests itself in the workplace. An older job applicant may be passed over for a younger one purely on the basis of age—since the older person is viewed as less capable—not because of an actual lack of experience or skills. At the other end of the spectrum, a company may try to coerce a long-time employee to go into retirement before he or she is ready in order to pay a new person less money to do the same job.

206. Which of the following statements is NOT supported by the passage?

(A) Ageism is discrimination against individuals or groups because of their age.

(B) Women also experience forms of benevolent prejudice.

(C) Many companies refuse to hire workers younger than eighteen.

(D) Ageism is frequently seen in the workforce.

(E) People with disabilities are often treated as though they cannot contribute to society.

207. As used in line 10, the word "ineptitude" most nearly means

(A) reluctance

(B) veraciousness

(C) divulgence

(D) incompetence

(E) omnipotence

208. According to the first paragraph, which of the following statements is true about ageism?

(A) The term "sexism" was coined in the mid-twentieth century.

(B) John McCain didn't win the presidency, because he was too old.

(C) There is more than one kind of age-related bias.

(D) Companies are allowed to promote the retirement of older workers.

(E) Senior citizens are disadvantaged and indolent.

209. As used in line 12, the word "manifests" most nearly means

(A) admires
(B) reveals
(C) circumnavigates
(D) abominates
(E) relinquishes

210. The author's attitude toward ageism can best be described as

(A) appalled
(B) delighted
(C) transcendental
(D) abrogated
(E) recrudescent

Passage 1

The image of women during wartime is primarily based on their presence on the home front, not on the front lines. Women were banned from enlistment in the U.S. military until well into the twentieth century, and until January 2013 were not permitted to serve in active combat.

Yet some women did not allow that restriction to stop them from fighting on 5 either the Union or Confederate side during the Civil War, even though both armies also prohibited their enlistment. Since it was illegal for them to fight on the battlefield, these brave and unconventional women embedded themselves in the army camps by concealing their gender. They changed their names and disguised themselves as men in order to become soldiers. Once enlisted and in the camps, it 10 was crucial to act and talk like a man to avert discovery.

But with a loose-fitting uniform, and with so many boy soldiers barely in their teens, it is not hard to see how a woman could live undetected for months or years. Their identities were often only discovered by accident—for example, one account tells of a woman who was discovered when she fell into a river and had to be res- 15 cued—or because of injury or death. A lucky few survived the war without ever being discovered. They served for years alongside their male counterparts and fought in many battles.

Some estimate the number of women who served in the Civil War to be nearly 1,000. Because they passed as men, it is impossible to know the exact number with 20 any certainty.

Passage 2

According to contemporary accounts, it was well known, both to male soldiers and to ordinary citizens, that women fought in the Union and Confederate armies. Stories by eyewitnesses and even published reports were common. In the case of one woman, Mary Owens, her triumphant return home after a serious injury was 25 widely celebrated in her town and featured in press coverage. She had enlisted in the Union army with her husband, William Evans, and carried on fighting after he had been killed in battle. She served for 18 months under the alias John Evans until treatment for her wounds revealed her gender. Stories of these women were often fodder for gossip in the army camps. 30

Decades after the war, many families included the details of these women's service in their obituaries. Articles about the soldier-women continued to be written. Unfortunately, the focus, and fascination, of the writers and the reading public appears not to have been with their heroic acts on the field, or with what life was like for them in the camps, but only with the fact that these women had enlisted 35 and whether or not they emerged from the war unscathed.

In addition, the U.S. government maintained information, during and after the war, of the existence of the soldier-women as part of the country's military archives. The U.S. Records and Pension Office kept complete service reports for a number of soldier-women, including discharge papers that list the cause for their 40 expulsion as the fact that their gender was discovered. In later years, some of these women even received a military pension for their service.

Despite such popular recognition, the Union and Confederate armies—and later the U.S. government—officially denied that any woman lived among the rank and file or that any woman had ever fought in the war. And because their stories were told in the general sphere and didn't find their way into school textbooks, the Civil War soldier-women are unknown to most Americans today.

45

211. The author's primary purpose in writing Passage 1 is to

(A) criticize the small number of women who fought in the Civil War
(B) expound on the reasons for the lack of women in combat
(C) bring to light the attitudes of citizens toward Civil War veterans
(D) describe the history of female soldiers in the Civil War
(E) justify the acceptance of boys as soldiers in the Civil War

212. As used in line 8 of Passage 1, the word "unconventional" most nearly means

(A) unusual
(B) virulent
(C) amateur
(D) licentious
(E) odious

213. With which of the following statements would the author of Passage 2 agree?

   I. The Union and Confederate armies were proud that women fought in the Civil War.
   II. The existence of soldier-women was no secret during or after the Civil War.
   III. Soldier-women of the Civil War accepted Victorian social constraints.

(A) I
(B) II
(C) I and II
(D) II and III
(E) III

214. The author of Passage 2 mentions Mary Owens in order to

(A) provide evidence of eyewitness accounts and published reports
(B) scrutinize the assertion that there were soldier-women in the Civil War
(C) imply that the majority of stories about soldier-women are false
(D) suggest that many eyewitness accounts cannot be trusted
(E) emphasize the racial inequality of the Union army

215. As used in line 33 of Passage 2, the word "fascination" most nearly means

(A) optimism
(B) putrescence
(C) gastronomy
(D) interest
(E) frailty

216. The authors of both passages discuss

(A) women who fought in the Union and Confederate armies
(B) the U.S. Records and Pension Office
(C) articles and obituaries of Civil War soldier-women
(D) boy soldiers under the age of fifteen
(E) the U.S. military in the twentieth century

217. In lines 12–13, the author of Passage 1 suggests reasons why

(A) the Union and Confederate armies prohibited women's enlistment
(B) so few women were wounded or killed in combat
(C) the U.S. Records and Pension Office kept complete service reports for soldier-women
(D) women were able to successfully pass as men in army camps
(E) some women died because their uniforms were too loose

218. The attitude of the author of Passage 1 toward women who fought in the Civil War can best be described as

(A) reverent
(B) onerous
(C) wearisome
(D) divisible
(E) heathenish

219. In lines 33–36 of Passage 2, the author implies that

(A) Mary Owens could have remained in service had she not been wounded

(B) specific details of these women's experiences were often not included in published accounts

(C) these women should never have received a military pension

(D) the identities of many soldier-women were only revealed in their obituaries

(E) the reading public was fascinated by the heroic acts of the soldier-women

220. As used in line 8 of Passage 1, the word "embedded" most nearly means

(A) garnished

(B) averted

(C) thwarted

(D) bewildered

(E) rooted

221. Which of the following statements most accurately describes the relationship between Passage 1 and Passage 2?

(A) Passage 1 is a direct rebuttal of the ideas in Passage 2.

(B) Both passages arrive at the same conclusion through different analyses.

(C) Passage 1 provides an alternative theory to that of Passage 2.

(D) The passages address different aspects of the same topic.

(E) Passage 2 provides the evidence to support the conclusions in Passage 1.

222. Which of the following best describes the "rank and file" mentioned in line 45 of Passage 2?

(A) The ordinary soldiers of an army, excluding the officers

(B) The tools and armaments of the armies

(C) The clothing and accessories worn by Victorian women

(D) The shackles and chains that held prisoners of war

(E) The uniforms worn by soldiers

223. As used in line 36 of Passage 2, the word "unscathed" most nearly means

(A) bestrewn

(B) unharmed

(C) clement

(D) formidable

(E) succinct

Urban planning as it is known today encompasses the development of land in the urban environment. It takes into account a number of factors, from transportation networks to the improvement and expansion of neighborhoods. Professionals in this line of work focus on the layout and architecture of the city, as well as on the patterns that emerge out of daily life. They frequently review or revise policies, 5 and they manage the preparation and construction of new projects.

One of the key issues that falls under the purview of urban planners is city traffic. Starting in the 1950s, urban planners required that construction companies provide generous plots for free parking spaces when they created commercial buildings. Today, urban planners require just the opposite, and building owners are 10 encouraged to charge for what few spaces are available. The intention of this policy is to force drivers to rely instead on mass transit, cycling, and walking when they go to urban spaces for work or leisure, thus creating less traffic congestion. So far, this has not proven to be the case. Therefore, building owners and city officials need to provide more incentives to get people out of their cars and onto their feet. 15

224. Which of the following statements best supports the author's conclusion?

(A) Urban planners did not take traffic into account when creating early parking strategies.

(B) People are less willing to drive into the city if they have to pay a lot for parking.

(C) Cyclists are required to wear protective gear and reflective clothing.

(D) People who don't drive their cars into urban centers are more conscientious regarding their health.

(E) Urban traffic flow is greatly reduced when there are fewer people driving into urban centers.

225. As used in line 13, the word "congestion" most nearly means

(A) overcrowding

(B) influenza

(C) subterfuge

(D) inherence

(E) dowry

226. The purpose of the first paragraph is to

(A) compare urban planning with civil engineering

(B) discuss the history of urban planning

(C) criticize the endeavors of urban planners

(D) indicate the pointlessness of urban planning

(E) describe what urban planners do

227. According to lines 3–5, one aspect of an urban planner's job would be to

(A) learn how to ride a bicycle

(B) design new police uniforms

(C) investigate the history of the automobile

(D) elect city officials to the city council

(E) research and analyze metropolitan routines

228. According to the passage, parking space requirements have changed since the 1950s because

(A) the number of cars, and therefore the amount of traffic, has decreased exponentially

(B) they are not safe options for cyclists and pedestrians

(C) modern improvements have made public transportation more attractive

(D) minimal free parking is supposed to prevent people from driving downtown

(E) they cause the terrible congestion experienced in most city centers

229. As used in line 7, the word "purview" most nearly means

(A) scope of responsibility

(B) special formality

(C) discriminating expression

(D) interval of time

(E) expression of thought

It was late November in 1456. The snow fell over Paris with rigorous, relentless persistence as the wind scattered it in flying, whirling vortices; sometimes there was a lull, and flake after flake descended out of the black night air—silent, circuitous, interminable.

To poor people, looking up under moist eyebrows, it seemed a wonder where 5
it all came from. Master Francis Villon had propounded alternatives at a tavern window earlier that day: Was it only the god Jupiter plucking geese on Olympus? Or were the holy angels molting? He was only a poor Master of Arts, and as the question somewhat touched upon divinity, he dared not venture to conclude. A silly old priest from Montargis, who was among the company, treated the young 10
rascal to a bottle of wine in honor of the jest and grimaces with which it was accompanied, and swore on his own white beard that he had been just such another irreverent dog when he was Villon's age.

The air was raw and pointed, though not far below freezing. The flakes were large, damp, and adhesive. The whole city was sheeted up. An army might have 15
marched from end to end and not a footfall given the alarm. If there were any belated birds in heaven, they saw Paris like a large white patch, and the bridges like slim white spars on the black ground of the river.

High up overhead the snow settled among the tracery of the cathedral towers. Many a niche was drifted full; many a statue wore a long white bonnet on its 20
grotesque or sainted head. The gargoyles had been transformed into great false noses, drooping toward the point. In the intervals of the wind, there was a dull sound dripping about the precincts of the church. The cemetery of St. John had taken its own share of the snow, as all the graves were decently covered.

In the distance, the tall white housetops stood around in grave array. Worthy 25
burghers were long ago in bed; there was no light in all the neighborhood, but a little peep from a lamp that hung swinging in the church choir and tossed the shadows to and fro in time to its oscillations. The patrol went by with halberds and a lantern, beating their hands; and they saw nothing suspicious about the cemetery of St. John. 30

Yet there was a small house, backed up against the cemetery wall, which was still awake, and awake to evil purpose, in that snoring district. There was not much to betray it from without; only a stream of warm vapor from the chimney top, a patch where the snow melted on the roof, and a few half-obliterated footprints at the door. But within, behind the shuttered windows, Master Francis Villon the 35
poet, and some of the thievish crew with whom he consorted, were keeping the night alive and passing round the bottle.

230. It can be inferred from the passage that the narrator is
- (A) the silly old priest
- (B) a third-party observer
- (C) St. John
- (D) a neighbor
- (E) Master Francis Villon

231. As used in line 4, the word "interminable" most nearly means

(A) bountiful
(B) disreputable
(C) palatial
(D) inconceivable
(E) endless

232. In the first paragraph, the narrator describes the snow falling on Paris as

(A) at times vigorous, other times lulled
(B) an unending torrent
(C) very light and almost invisible
(D) passing by rather quickly
(E) not sticking on the ground

233. The narrator would most likely agree that "poor people, looking up under moist eyebrows" (line 5)

(A) had just taken a swim in the Seine River
(B) had the misfortune of being outside on such a cold, snowy night
(C) were uncomfortable because they were firmly against taking baths
(D) could not afford anything to drink
(E) were mourners from a funeral and had been crying

234. As used in line 6, the word "propounded" most nearly means

(A) caroused
(B) suggested
(C) deteriorated
(D) vexed
(E) stifled

235. Villon is described as an "irreverent dog" because his "alternative" theories on the snow

(A) were sinful and impious speculation
(B) described a raucous scene
(C) were highly improbable
(D) were based on an idea about stray dogs
(E) implied that he had rabies

236. As used in line 14, the phrase "raw and pointed" means that

    (A) the men were supposed to have a fencing lesson

    (B) the snow had hardened and was dangerous

    (C) the men had decided to meet at the butcher shop

    (D) bandits were hurting people outside

    (E) the air outside was bitterly cold

237. As used in line 21, the word "grotesque" most nearly means

    (A) tireless

    (B) restrained

    (C) hideous

    (D) doleful

    (E) blithe

238. The narrator's description of the cathedral statues suggests that they

    (A) had been dressed for a ceremony

    (B) were actually a person standing very still

    (C) had been blessed by the church

    (D) were covered in snow

    (E) represented the angels in heaven

239. As used in line 24, the word "decently" most nearly means

    (A) courteously

    (B) demurely

    (C) impolitely

    (D) abundantly

    (E) responsibly

240. Based on the context of the fifth paragraph (lines 25–30), the word "burghers" most nearly means

    (A) citizens of a town

    (B) patties of ground beef

    (C) cattle and oxen

    (D) small children

    (E) marble statues

241. The tone of the passage can best be described as

(A) ungainly
(B) ominous
(C) vociferous
(D) tenuous
(E) mandatory

242. The author mentions the scene with the lamp and the church (lines 26–28) in order to

(A) indicate the critical importance of the church
(B) underscore how deserted the town was at that hour
(C) provide a setting for the funeral at the cemetery
(D) clarify how it was used to guide lost travelers
(E) imply that the men on patrol were in danger

243. The purpose of the last paragraph is to

(A) illustrate how profoundly dark the night was
(B) emphasize how dangerous the neighborhood was
(C) provide an alibi for Villon's brother
(D) explain the setting in the cemetery
(E) imply that the people inside were devising a wicked plan

244. Which of the following statements best describes the reason for the half-obliterated footprints mentioned in line 34?

(A) The patrol men had stepped over them during their rounds.
(B) The snow had melted away.
(C) Villon and his friends had been inside the house for a while.
(D) The snowstorm was all in Villon's mind.
(E) The dog trampled on them while he played in the snow.

245. Which of the following statements is/are NOT supported by the passage?
  I. Villon and his friends were up late, plotting a scheme.
  II. Villon and his friends had been drinking all day.
  III. Villon and his friends were about to become priests.

(A) I
(B) II
(C) II and III
(D) III
(E) I and II

Russell Williams Porter was one of several explorers at the turn of the twentieth century who ventured into the alien regions above the Arctic Circle in a quest to reach the North Pole. Born in 1871 in Vermont, Porter studied architecture and art at the world-renowned Massachusetts Institute of Technology before beginning his career as an explorer. 5

He made six voyages between 1894 and 1903 to various areas around the Arctic, and left an impressive collection of paintings, drawings, notebooks, journals, and correspondence. His expeditions included trips to Greenland and Alaska with the famed explorer Frederick Cook.

Porter's drawings are beautifully detailed representations of the people and 10 landscape of the North, as well as incomparable scientific documentation of the journeys. Many of the sketches were drawn in subzero temperatures, making the Porter collection a true testament to his skill and stamina.

246. As used in line 2, the word "alien" most nearly means

(A) unknown
(B) extraterrestrial
(C) outlandish
(D) predictable
(E) devastating

247. The narrator mentions Porter's educational background to

(A) contrast it with that of Frederick Cook
(B) illustrate how isolationist he was
(C) criticize his aristocratic upbringing
(D) indicate his lack of proficiency
(E) help explain why his drawings were so exceptional

248. The word that best describes the author's attitude toward Porter is

(A) contempt
(B) embolism
(C) paramount
(D) admiration
(E) pedestrian

249. The main point of the passage is that

(A) Frederick Cook deserved more recognition as an explorer
(B) the Massachusetts Institute of Technology is a remarkable school
(C) a number of great explorers were born in Vermont
(D) Porter was both a gifted artist and fearless explorer
(E) Greenland and Alaska are cold and formidable places

250. Which of the following statements can be inferred from the last paragraph?

(A) Porter was compelled to make the treacherous journey by his family.

(B) Researching North Pole expeditions means coming face to face with the past.

(C) One can appreciate Porter's sketches and paintings on many levels.

(D) The Porter collection also contains invaluable photographs.

(E) The Porter collection is a national treasure that has been lost to the ages.

Directly in front of him, holding on by a low branch, stood a naked brown baby who could just walk. He looked up into Father Wolf's face, and laughed.

"How little! How naked, and—how bold!" said Mother Wolf softly.

The moonlight was suddenly blocked out of the mouth of the cave, for Shere Khan's great square head and shoulders were thrust into the entrance.   5

"Shere Khan does us great honor," said Father Wolf, but his eyes were very angry. "What does Shere Khan need?"

"A man's cub went this way. Its parents have run off. Give it to me." The tiger filled the cave with thunder.

Mother Wolf shook herself clear of the cubs and sprang forward, her eyes, like   10 two green moons in the darkness, facing the blazing eyes of Shere Khan.

"And it is I, Raksha the Demon, who answers. The man's cub is mine. He shall not be killed."

Father Wolf looked on amazed. He had almost forgotten the days when he won Mother Wolf in fair fight from five other wolves, when she ran in the Pack and was   15 not called The Demon for compliment's sake.

Shere Khan might have faced Father Wolf, but he could not stand up against Mother Wolf, for he knew that where he was, she had all the advantage of the ground, and would fight to the death. So he backed out of the cave mouth growling. He would concoct a plan.   20

Mother Wolf threw herself down panting among the cubs, and Father Wolf said to her gravely: "Wilt thou really keep him, Mother?"

251. The author uses the expression "filled the cave with thunder" (line 9) to mean that Shere Khan

(A) was a wizard with magical powers
(B) roared loudly
(C) brought a lamp
(D) pushed two boulders together
(E) attacked Father Wolf

252. It can be inferred from lines 4–7 that Shere Khan

(A) didn't recognize Father Wolf
(B) was highly respected and feared
(C) was unnaturally large for a tiger
(D) could not take his eyes off Mother Wolf
(E) was going to eat the wolf cubs

253. In the descriptions of Mother Wolf, the narrator implies that she

(A) could not leave her cubs
(B) suffered from amnesia
(C) had run away from her pack
(D) was a first-time mother
(E) was a brave, fearsome fighter

254. According to the ninth paragraph (lines 17–20), all of the following are reasons why Shere Khan left the wolves EXCEPT

(A) He couldn't fit in the cave.
(B) Mother Wolf would use her position to her advantage.
(C) The cubs would be in danger during the fight.
(D) Mother Wolf would fight to the death.
(E) He decided to get the human baby some other way.

255. As used in line 22, the word "gravely" most nearly means

(A) solemnly
(B) obnoxiously
(C) effervescently
(D) ungainly
(E) virulently

Passage 1

During the Spanish-American War, the Marine Corps began its development into the stealthy, well-oiled machine that it is known as today. Ironically, the sinking of the USS *Maine*, a battleship that was sent to Cuba to protect American interests in the region against Spanish aggression, served as a catalyst for bringing the two nations to war. 5

As aggression escalated, the Marine Corps was substantially prepared and displayed something future Marines would take pride in—the ability to be called upon and respond at a moment's notice. The Marine Corps seized the base at Guantanamo Bay, Cuba, which was still in use by the U.S. military in the 2010s. The Corps also led the American forces in the Philippines, Guam, and Puerto 10 Rico, all of which became U.S. territories. After the war, naval bases in these new territories meant U.S. ships could successfully operate worldwide.

Passage 2

At the end of the Spanish-American War, a number of territories under Spanish sovereignty were ceded to the U.S. under the Treaty of Paris. Among them was Puerto Rico, which remains a U.S. territory to this day. 15

Since Puerto Ricans have been U.S. citizens since 1917, they have a long history of service in the U.S. armed forces. They have served in every major U.S. military campaign of the twentieth century. Soon after becoming American citizens, roughly 20,000 Puerto Rican soldiers were sent to fight in World War I. They were stationed along the Western Front in France and quickly earned a reputation 20 among the enemy as fierce fighters.

After World War I, Puerto Ricans were assigned to conflicts around the world as members of the U.S. Marine Corps. In one conflict in the mid-1920s, part of the so-called Banana Wars, 3,000 U.S. Marines were quickly sent to Nicaragua, then embroiled in a civil war, in order to protect American citizens there. It is esti- 25 mated that more than 65,000 Puerto Ricans served in World War II, both in Europe and in the Pacific theater. Tens of thousands also served in the Korean War, the Vietnam War, the Gulf War, and most recently the campaigns in Iraq and Afghanistan.

In every conflict, Puerto Rican soldiers have bravely protected the United 30 States and its interests abroad, earning awards and recognition for their courage—and sometimes making the ultimate sacrifice.

256. Which one of the following statements can be inferred from Passage 1?

(A) The Treaty of Paris was considered entirely unfair by the Spanish government.

(B) The commander of the First Marine Battalion had decades of experience in the Marine Corps.

(C) The Marine Corps played a very large role in the military conflicts of the twentieth century.

(D) The Marine Corps was beloved by the American public.

(E) The Marine Corps had a low rate of disease and sickness, compared to that found in army units.

257. The author's primary purpose in writing Passage 2 is to

(A) describe the history of Puerto Ricans serving in the U.S. military

(B) criticize the inclusion of Puerto Ricans in the draft

(C) illustrate how large the Puerto Rican population is in the northeastern United States

(D) explain the large number of Puerto Rican veterans in California

(E) justify the annexation of Puerto Rico by the United States

258. Which of the following statements best describes the "something" mentioned in line 7 of Passage 1?

(A) The Corps also led the American forces in the Philippines, Guam, and Puerto Rico.

(B) The Spanish-American War demonstrated the fast mobilization of the Marine Corps.

(C) The Marine Corps was useless as a fighting force in the Pacific Ocean.

(D) The U.S. Navy became responsible for active operations worldwide.

(E) The Spanish-American War expanded the number of U.S. territories.

259. Which of the following statements most accurately describes the relationship between Passage 1 and Passage 2?

(A) Passage 1 is a direct rebuttal of the ideas in Passage 2.

(B) Both passages arrive at the same conclusion through different analyses.

(C) Passage 1 provides an alternative theory to that of Passage 2.

(D) The passages discuss the same topics, but they focus on different aspects of the topics.

(E) Passage 2 provides the evidence to support the conclusions in Passage 1.

260. The author's attitude toward Puerto Ricans in the military in Passage 2 can best be described as

(A) condescending
(B) indifferent
(C) complimentary
(D) exasperated
(E) understanding

261. With which of the following statements about the USS *Maine* would the author of Passage 1 most likely agree?

(A) The explosion of the USS *Maine* eventually led Congress to declare war on Spain in 1898.
(B) The cause of the explosion of the USS *Maine* was never established.
(C) The USS *Maine* was a world-class, state-of-the-art battleship.
(D) The USS *Maine* never should have been sent to Cuba.
(E) The USS *Maine* was sent to Nicaragua during a bitter civil war.

262. The author of Passage 1 uses the expression "well-oiled machine" (line 2) to mean that

(A) the battleships of the nineteenth century were ineffective
(B) American citizens were not in any danger before the war
(C) the Marine Corps has become powerful and efficient
(D) the skills of the Marine Corps took time to develop
(E) Cuba had large crude oil deposits

263. With which of the following statements would the authors of both passages agree?

(A) Puerto Ricans were made U.S. citizens so that they could be drafted in World War I.
(B) The bravery of the Marine Corps was evident during the highly tense battles of the Korean War.
(C) The Marine Corps did not respond quickly enough to the Banana War conflicts.
(D) Guantanamo Bay is an essential military base for the United States.
(E) The Marines would play a vital role in future conflicts both in the Pacific Ocean and in Europe.

264. As used in line 14 of Passage 2, the word "sovereignty" most nearly means

(A) monarchy
(B) trepidation
(C) reproach
(D) control
(E) cacophony

265. In line 32 of Passage 2, "ultimate sacrifice" is symbolic of

(A) giving up a medal of honor
(B) giving your life for your country
(C) running from the draft
(D) fighting the Germans
(E) being assigned to new conflicts

It has been clearly documented that crime levels in the United States have been falling for some time. In fact, crime levels today are at their lowest level since the 1960s. Adding positive news to these statistics is that many states are heeding the call for reforms in sentencing and corrections procedures. The goal of these reforms is not only to keep people out of prison, but to enhance the efficacy of the parole 5 system, for example, by helping to provide adequate housing or employment to convicted felons.

Notwithstanding these efforts, it is also well known that the jail population of the United States has grown to an alarming size. Studies have shown that one of the reasons for this dramatic increase is the war on drugs, since a citizen can be 10 arrested for the possession of minute amounts of an illegal substance.

This increase has had the most dire consequences in African-American communities, where males are six times more likely to be incarcerated than white males. This statistic is also true of black women, whose incarceration rate is four times that of white females. 15

There is also an aging prison population in this nation, due to the fact that people are serving more time than those in past decades. More than 120,000 people are serving life sentences, and nearly 25 percent of those people do not have the possibility of parole.

It is evident that the current measures to substantially reduce the U.S. jail 20 population are a step in the right direction, but are not enough. City and state officials must come together to brainstorm new solutions and put forward more reforms.

266. Which of the following statements best supports the main point of the passage?

    (A) Local communities are often hardest hit by this dire situation.
    (B) Men and boys are the face of drug crimes in America.
    (C) Most people serving life sentences have the possibility of parole.
    (D) There are more people in jail today than there were 20 years ago.
    (E) Convicted felons usually have few, if any, job skills.

267. As used in line 5, the word "efficacy" most nearly means

    (A) degree
    (B) competence
    (C) calumny
    (D) novice
    (E) remission

268. In the third paragraph (lines 12–15), the author suggests that

(A) the increase of incarceration in America is felt most strongly by minorities

(B) men are much more likely to be sentenced on drug charges

(C) women are receiving ineffective or incompetent counsel in the first stages of the criminal justice system

(D) Hispanics are the second-largest minority group in U.S. prisons

(E) jails in Asia and South America are often semiautonomous societies

269. The first paragraph serves mostly to

(A) exculpate the failures of the U.S. judicial system

(B) disavow the practices of judges in the 1960s

(C) explain the current state of U.S. corrections procedures

(D) provide evidence for the need for the war on drugs

(E) warn against the consequences of a felony record

270. The author mentions the aging prison population in order to

(A) emphasize the insidious nature of Alzheimer's disease

(B) imply that senior citizens are committing more crimes

(C) provide another reason for the current U.S. jail population crisis

(D) protest the abolition of the death penalty in most states

(E) suggest that prisoners over sixty-five years old should be pardoned

Trichromacy results when an organism's retina contains three types of receptor cells to perceive color, specifically, blue, green, and red pigments. In humans and closely related primates, this may have been inherited from our very early vertebrate ancestors millions of years ago. For example, fish and birds use more than three pigments for vision. It is believed that two of these pigments were lost as most mammals evolved. But somewhere along the evolutionary chain, one additional cell was reacquired.   5

Most other mammals, except for marsupials, are currently thought to be dichromats; they can see only blue and green pigments. Dichromacy occurs in humans as well; it is hereditary and predominantly affects males.   10

The current theory for humans becoming trichromats has to do with food. The colors of ripe fruit frequently stand out against the surrounding foliage. Those animals that were able to distinguish red fruit and young leaves from other vegetation were able to consume more food and successfully bear offspring. The ability to identify ripe fruit, therefore, led to greater numbers of animals with trichromatic traits.   15

271. It can be inferred from the passage that

(A) trichromats can detect more colors than dichromats
(B) dichromacy is common in fish and birds
(C) monochromacy is preferable to trichromacy
(D) most carnivores are dichromats
(E) dichromats consume more food

272. In lines 3–6, the author suggests that

(A) fish, birds, and humans eventually went down different evolutionary paths
(B) humans could evolve to have red eyes
(C) fish, birds, and humans have 20/20 vision
(D) higher intelligence is required for complex vision
(E) fish and birds have too many pigments that are no longer useful

273. According to the passage, which of the following statements is/are true about dichromacy?
   I. Dichromats can perceive as many as 10,000 different colors.
   II. Dichromacy, referred to as color blindness, can be present in human females.
   III. Dichromats can see only blue and green pigments.
   (A) I
   (B) II
   (C) I and II
   (D) III
   (E) II and III

274. Which of the following statements would most undermine the author's conclusion about the role of ripe fruit in trichromacy?
   (A) Predators lowered the number of trichromats in a given area.
   (B) Genetic mutation was required for animals to become trichromats.
   (C) Detecting skin flushing, and thereby mood, may have influenced trichromatic vision.
   (D) There is a direct correlation between survival rate and hair color.
   (E) Trichromats are more intelligent than dichromats.

275. As used in line 13, the word "distinguish" most nearly means
   (A) exhort
   (B) celebrate
   (C) tantalize
   (D) suppress
   (E) differentiate

The term "telecommuting" refers to a workforce arrangement in which there is no central office where employees gather and work. Instead, these employees work wherever they can access the people and materials needed to complete their projects and daily tasks. One of the most common locations for telecommuters to work is their own homes. However, with today's advanced technological equip- 5 ment, employees can work anywhere. Laptop computers and tablets allow for facile mobility, as do wireless Internet "hot spots" and even smartphones with high-speed Internet connectivity.

More employers should consider the advantages of a telecommuting arrange- ment. It allows employers to hire people who otherwise would not be available. 10 This includes parents with small children, the physically disabled, and people liv- ing far from urban centers. Plus, it allows for a more globalized business, since the company can employ people in all parts of the world, regardless of location or time zone. According to a recent poll, approximately one in five workers telecommutes frequently, and nearly 10 percent never set foot in a traditional office. 15

Still, some barriers do exist to more employers' adopting a telecommuting work model. Liability insurance and worker's compensation in case of accidents can become serious issues, and all other applicable laws and regulations must be fully investigated. In addition, the long-established way to manage employees has been to observe workers firsthand. Therefore, many companies do not allow full- 20 time telecommuting for fear of a drop in productivity levels.

However, most studies find that frequent face-to-face interactions through video-conferencing, as well as allowing for periods of adjustment to the new work regime, are often all that is needed to overcome any obstacles. The advantages of telecommuting—even two or three days a week—far outweigh any possible draw- 25 backs, and most of the employer concerns about telecommuting are unfounded. They are simply based on ignorance of new hi-tech breakthroughs or on apprehen- sion of change to the traditional workforce environment. Clearly, employers today should not overlook the option of telecommuting.

276. The conclusion of the passage is best supported by all of the following statements EXCEPT

(A) Telecommuting increases employee output and reduces employee absences.

(B) Employers can set up inexpensive "hot desks" anywhere with a laptop, an Internet connection, and a phone.

(C) Telecommuting helps the environment, since people would not have to drive their cars or use other modes of transportation to go to work every day.

(D) Workers who begin as telecommuters may eventually prefer self-employment.

(E) Telecommuting has many financial benefits, such as lower operating expenses.

277. The main point of the second paragraph (lines 9–15) is that

(A) virtual offices are not confined to the home
(B) telecommuting reduces rent and electricity costs
(C) telecommuting has numerous benefits
(D) globalized businesses are more lucrative
(E) living far from urban centers is no longer a problem

278. The author's attitude toward telecommuting can be described as

(A) supercilious
(B) enthusiastic
(C) gracious
(D) frustrated
(E) apathetic

279. The author's primary purpose in writing the passage is to

(A) describe the technical terms used by telecommuters
(B) disparage the greed of companies that do not allow telecommuting
(C) explain the reasons why some companies do not permit telecommuting
(D) excuse the lack of technology to aid in improving telecommuting
(E) extol the merits of telecommuting

280. With which of the following statements would the author most likely agree?

(A) Companies considering telecommuting should check on legal issues, union rules, and zoning laws.
(B) There are no serious obstacles in organizations' attempting to adopt telecommuting.
(C) Twenty-five percent of all companies that allow telecommuting discontinue the practice after one year.
(D) The only way to make telecommuting more common is to make video-conferencing mandatory for all companies.
(E) Telecommuting should not be allowed for fewer than three days a week.

281. As used in line 7, the word "facile" most nearly means

(A) easy
(B) profound
(C) complementary
(D) bountiful
(E) expeditious

The history of the Portuguese Empire is often overshadowed by the empires of England and Spain, yet the Portuguese established the first global empire in history. Spanning nearly six centuries, it began in 1415 with the conquest of Ceuta, off the north coast of Africa, and did not officially end until 1999, when Macau, located across from Hong Kong, was handed over to the Chinese government. Territories in more than 50 countries were at some point ruled by the Portuguese.   5

The empire began as a result of the unparalleled skill of Portuguese sailors, who took to the high seas at the very start of the fifteenth century, hoping to find a way to dominate the ultraprofitable spice trade. They were expert navigators, skilled mapmakers, and knowledgeable operators of new maritime equipment. Some of   10 the most famous early explorers were Bartolomeu Dias, who rounded Africa's Cape of Good Hope in 1488, and Vasco da Gama, famous for finding an alternate route to India in 1498.

By the late-1500s, the Portuguese had established settlements in every corner of the globe. Eventually, Portugal's network was too vast and too prosperous to sur-   15 vive the ambitions of countries such as Spain, the Netherlands, Britain, and France, and the Portuguese Empire began its slow but steady decline.

282. Which of the following statements is NOT supported by the passage?

(A) The empire's commercial network brought great wealth to Portugal.
(B) Portuguese colonies became the subject of attacks by rival European powers.
(C) Portuguese sailors explored the coasts of nearly all the continents.
(D) The Portuguese were the last Europeans to enter the spice trade.
(E) By the twentieth century, the empire had dwindled to a handful of territories.

283. It can be inferred from the passage that

(A) Pedro Álvares Cabral discovered Brazil on the South American coast
(B) between 1580 and 1640, Portugal became a partner with Spain
(C) the Portuguese used recent developments in maritime technology to their advantage
(D) the Portuguese had a trade monopoly in the Indian Ocean
(E) Indonesia invaded East Timor in 1975, ending Portuguese rule

284. According to the passage, which of the following statements was an advantage of the Portuguese sailors?
    (A) Bartolomeu Dias aided in the construction of the ship that Vasco da Gama took to India.
    (B) The Cape of Good Hope was famous for its deadly storms.
    (C) They made sure to stop at friendly ports during long voyages.
    (D) They had immense success because of their remarkable proficiency in cartography.
    (E) Once Pedro Álvares Cabral discovered Brazil, all other destinations were easy to find.

285. The purpose of the last paragraph is to
    (A) absolve the president of Portugal of war crimes
    (B) commend the accomplishments of Portuguese sailors
    (C) demonstrate how vast the Spanish Empire was
    (D) condemn the acts of all colonial powers
    (E) explain the causes of the Portuguese Empire's inexorable deterioration

From the table at which they had been lunching, two American ladies of ripe but well-cared-for middle age moved across the lofty terrace of the Roman restaurant and, leaning on its parapet, looked first at each other, and then down on the outspread glories of the Palatine and the Forum, with the same expression of vague but benevolent approval.

The luncheon hour was long past, and the two had their end of the vast terrace to themselves. At its opposite extremity, a few groups, detained by a lingering look at the outspread city, were gathering up guidebooks and fumbling for tips. The last of them scattered, and the two ladies were alone on the air-washed height.

"Well, I don't see why we shouldn't just stay here," said Mrs. Slade, the lady of the high color and energetic brows. Two derelict basket chairs stood near, and she pushed them into the angle of the parapet, and settled herself in one, her gaze upon the Palatine. "After all, it's still the most beautiful view in the world."

"It always will be, to me," assented her friend Mrs. Ansley, with so slight a stress on the "me" that Mrs. Slade, though she noticed it, wondered if it were not merely accidental, like the random underlinings of old-fashioned letter writers.

"Grace Ansley was always old-fashioned," she thought, and added aloud, with a retrospective smile: "It's a view we've both been familiar with for a good many years. When we first met here, we were younger than our girls are now. You remember!"

"Oh, yes, I remember," murmured Mrs. Ansley, with the same indefinable stress—"There's that headwaiter wondering," she interpolated. She was evidently far less sure of herself and of her rights in the world than Mrs. Slade.

"I'll cure him of wondering," said Mrs. Slade, stretching her hand toward a bag as opulent-looking as Mrs. Ansley's. Signing to the headwaiter, she explained that she and her friend were old lovers of Rome and would like to spend the end of the afternoon looking down on the view—that is, if it did not disturb the service! The headwaiter, bowing over her gratuity, assured her that the ladies were most welcome, and would be still more so if they would condescend to remain for dinner. A full-moon night they would remember. . . .

Mrs. Slade's black brows drew together, as though references to the moon were out of place and even unwelcome. But she smiled away her frown as the headwaiter retreated. "Well, why not! We might do worse. There's no knowing, I suppose, when the girls will be back. Do you even know back from where? I don't!"

Mrs. Ansley again colored slightly. "I think those young Italian aviators we met at the embassy invited them to fly to Tarquinia for tea. I suppose they'll want to wait and fly back by moonlight."

"Moonlight—moonlight! What a part it still plays in the lives of young lovers. Do you suppose they're as sentimental as we were?"

"I've come to the conclusion that I don't in the least know what they are," said Mrs. Ansley. "And perhaps we didn't know much more about each other."

"No, perhaps we didn't."

Her friend gave her a shy glance. "I never should have supposed you were sentimental, Alida."

286. In lines 1–2, the narrator uses the phrase "ripe but well-cared-for" to describe

(A) the restaurant
(B) the ladies at lunch
(C) the tomato plants
(D) the luggage
(E) the automobile

287. As used in line 3, the word "parapet" most nearly means

(A) nemesis
(B) harangue
(C) denouement
(D) zephyr
(E) wall

288. The narrator's description of the people in lines 7–8 suggests that they are

(A) policemen
(B) pilots
(C) tourists
(D) actors
(E) chauffeurs

289. It can be inferred from the passage that the scene takes place

(A) in the late afternoon
(B) early in the morning
(C) in the middle of the night
(D) at dinnertime
(E) in the moonlight

290. As used in line 7, the word "extremity" most nearly means

(A) bulwark
(B) edge
(C) limb
(D) epitome
(E) nadir

291. The conversation in lines 10–21 serves mostly to

(A) introduce the headwaiter to the daughters
(B) explain what the ladies were doing at the restaurant
(C) scold the young Italian aviators they met at the embassy
(D) give details about the relationship between Mrs. Slade and Mrs. Ansley
(E) justify the fact that this was their second visit to Rome that year

292. In the comparison in lines 22–23, the narrator suggests that

(A) Mrs. Ansley resents Mrs. Slade because Mrs. Slade is a younger woman
(B) Mrs. Slade would much rather be in Rome without Mrs. Ansley
(C) Mrs. Ansley doesn't trust the aviators around her daughter
(D) Mrs. Ansley is blond, while Mrs. Slade is brunette
(E) Mrs. Slade is more gregarious and confident than Mrs. Ansley

293. Mrs. Slade has a retrospective smile, because she is

(A) recalling the past
(B) masking her umbrage
(C) unable to laugh
(D) unhappily married
(E) cautiously optimistic

294. In line 25, the narrator uses the phrase "as opulent-looking as Mrs. Ansley's" to suggest that

(A) both ladies are well-to-do women in society
(B) Mrs. Slade is tagging along with her wealthier friend
(C) their daughters are very fashionable girls
(D) they are in desperate need of a hotel room
(E) Mrs. Slade enjoys traveling with her friend

295. In the seventh paragraph (lines 24–30), the narrator implies that Mrs. Slade

(A) does not approve of Mrs. Ansley's old-fashioned notions
(B) addresses the headwaiter condescendingly
(C) gives the headwaiter some money as a bribe so they can stay there longer
(D) decided that it would be best for the group that she pay for tomorrow's lunch in advance
(E) did not bring enough money with her to pay for lunch

296. In line 22, the narrator suggests that Mrs. Ansley's comment was

    (A) never meant to have been heard by Mrs. Slade

    (B) an interruption of Mrs. Slade's recollections of their past together in Rome

    (C) considered by Mrs. Slade to have been extremely rude

    (D) spoken by Mrs. Ansley to show she was not impressed with the service

    (E) overheard by the tourists at the other end of the terrace

297. As used in line 33, the word "retreated" most nearly means

    (A) sashayed

    (B) atoned

    (C) withdrew

    (D) fled

    (E) wrangled

298. In the last sentence, Mrs. Ansley reveals that she is surprised because

    (A) the last time they had been together in Rome, they fought

    (B) Mrs. Slade was in deep mourning for her recently deceased husband

    (C) her daughter no longer wanted to be friends with Mrs. Slade's daughter

    (D) she did not think Mrs. Slade would be emotional about their youthful adventures

    (E) the time had passed so quickly since they finished lunch

299. In the passage, the moonlight is used by the author as a symbol of

    (A) ancient Rome

    (B) the bustle of the city

    (C) airplanes and navigation

    (D) changing ocean tides

    (E) youth and romance

300. As used in line 44, the word "sentimental" most nearly means

    (A) maudlin

    (B) concurrent

    (C) orthodox

    (D) ignoble

    (E) nonpareil

CHAPTER **4**

Set 4 Questions

London was the first city to have an underground railway system to move both people and goods. The Metropolitan Railway, or the "Met," was opened to the public in 1863, and its tracks spanned all the way from the city's financial center to today's Middlesex suburbs. The railway was necessary because of the immense population explosion in London that 5 occurred at the beginning of the nineteenth century. Gas-lit wooden carriages were moved along the line by steam locomotives.

The railway brought a number of transformations to city life in London. First, it made the city more traversable for the masses. Second, it brought about the urbanization of the London suburbs. When the Met 10 did not use land it had bought for tracks or rail yards, it sponsored development of the property, known as Metro-land, for other uses, primarily reasonably priced housing.

The Met line moved forward with the turn of the twentieth century. For example, electric traction was introduced in 1905. By the mid-1930s, 15 the Metropolitan Railway was incorporated into the larger public transportation system of the city, which included buses and trams. Today, London's train system is known simply as the Underground.

301. With which of the following statements would the author likely agree?

(A) As London's streets filled with more people, a sophisticated public transportation system was required.

(B) The Met, built and opened in 1863, is one of the world's greatest museums.

(C) London's suburbs were once well connected, but today are only accessible by car.

(D) The land used for train tracks or rail yards was inhospitable and deserted.

(E) The building of the Met underground railway system bankrupted Britain.

302. It can be inferred from lines 17–18 that

(A) people in the twenty-first century no longer use public transportation
(B) the brand name "the Met" eventually fell out of use
(C) Londoners prefer to use buses and trams
(D) the first trams were established in London as well
(E) using public transportation was frowned on in the 1930s

303. The author mentions the changes in lines 15–17 in order to

(A) suggest that the Met had long since fallen into disrepair
(B) emphasize the size of the Met railway system
(C) provide evidence that the Met was still the only railway system in Europe
(D) explain how frequently people were using the Met
(E) imply that the owners of the Met made improvements as technology improved

304. According to the passage, London was transformed because of

(A) the sudden but inevitable onset of World War II
(B) long-standing agreements between bus and tram systems
(C) American innovations such as the steam engine and cinema
(D) a new wave of immigrants from mainland Europe
(E) accessible rapid transit and affordable housing

305. As used in line 16, the word "incorporated" most nearly means

(A) formalized
(B) ostracized
(C) caroused
(D) integrated
(E) reprimanded

Pinguicula moranensis, found in tropical parts of Mexico and Guatemala, is a remarkable insectivorous plant. Vegetation like *Pinguicula moranensis* is known to digest insects, because the soil on which they grow is devoid of the nutrients they require to thrive.

In the summertime, *Pinguicula moranensis* forms a flowerlike "rosette" with its 5 leaves; this structure can be up to four inches long. Covering these broad leaves are glands that secrete a sticky substance that attracts insects. *Pinguicula moranensis* is then able to digest the arthropods.

In the winter months, when its regular diet of insects is not available and water is scarce, *Pinguicula moranensis* conserves energy by growing a beautiful noninsec- 10 tivorous flower that resembles an orchid, forming just one bud at the end of a long stalk. The flower comes in various shades of pink and purple, and appears just once or twice a year.

The species was first observed and collected more than 300 years ago by the famous explorers Alexander von Humboldt and Aimé Bonpland. It remains a pop- 15 ular plant for cultivation due to its insectivorous properties and delightful flower.

306. It can be inferred from the passage that *Pinguicula moranensis* is insectivorous, because

(A) it consumes insects

(B) it looks like an insect

(C) it has the same DNA as some insects

(D) it has a symbiotic relationship with insects

(E) it was first discovered by insect experts

307. As used in line 8, "arthropods" is another word for

(A) plants

(B) insects

(C) flowers

(D) explorers

(E) leaves

308. In lines 2–4, the author suggests that

(A) the soil contains too much mercury

(B) *Pinguicula moranensis* requires a particular kind of insect

(C) the insects provide nutrients that the soil cannot

(D) *Pinguicula moranensis* can grow only in Mexico and Guatemala

(E) irrigation in major cities has all but wiped out *Pinguicula moranensis*

309. The author's tone can best be described as

(A) listless

(B) granular

(C) delectable

(D) concurrent

(E) passionate

310. Which of the following statements is NOT supported by the passage?

(A) *Pinguicula moranensis* has been a popular plant for cultivation for hundreds of years.

(B) Native insects are drawn to the plant, get stuck on the leaves, and are trapped.

(C) Insectivorous plants derive some or most of their nutrients from insects.

(D) Plants that digest insects do so using various methods, such as pitcherlike formations.

(E) *Pinguicula moranensis* conserves energy in winter, producing its flower just once or twice a year.

It was a dull New England town; no one could deny that, for everybody was so intensely proper and well-born that nobody dared to be jolly. All the houses were square, aristocratic mansions with Revolutionary elms in front and spacious coach-houses behind. The knockers had a supercilious perk to their bronze or brass noses—as though they knew they had been there since the war for independence— 5 the dandelions on the lawns had a highly connected air, and the very pigs were evidently descended from "our first families." Stately dinner-parties, decorous dances, moral picnics, and much tea-pot gossiping were the social resources of the place. Of course, the young people flirted, for that diversion is apparently irradicable even in the "best society," but it was done with a propriety which was 10 edifying to behold.

One can easily imagine that such a starched state of things would not be particularly attractive to a travelled young gentleman like Lennox, who, as Kate very truly said, had been spoilt by the flattery, luxury, and gayety of foreign society. He did his best, but by the end of the first week ennui claimed him for its own, and 15 passive endurance was all that was left him. From perfect despair he was rescued by the scarlet stockings, which went tripping by one day as he stood at the window, planning some means of escape.

A brisk, blithe-faced girl passed in a gray walking suit with a distracting pair of high-heeled boots and glimpses of scarlet at the ankle. Modest, perfectly so, I 20 assure you, were the glimpses; but the feet were so decidedly pretty that one forgot to look at the face appertaining thereunto. It wasn't a remarkably lovely face, but it was a happy, wholesome one, with all sorts of good little dimples in cheek and chin, sunshiny twinkles in the black eyes, and a decided, yet lovable look about the mouth that was quite satisfactory. A busy, bustling little body she seemed to be, for 25 sack-pockets and muff were full of bundles, and the trim boots tripped briskly over the ground, as if the girl's heart were as light as her heels. Somehow this active, pleasant figure seemed to wake up the whole street, and leave a streak of sunshine behind it, for every one nodded as it passed, and the primmest faces relaxed into smiles, which lingered when the girl had gone. 30

"Uncommonly pretty feet,—she walks well, which American girls seldom do,—all waddle or prance,—nice face, but the boots are French, and it does my heart good to see them."

Lennox made these observations to himself as the young lady approached, nodded to Kate at another window, gave a quick but comprehensive glance at 35 himself and trotted round the corner, leaving the impression on his mind that a whiff of fresh spring air had blown through the street in spite of the December snow. He didn't trouble himself to ask who it was, but fell into the way of lounging in the bay-window at about three PM, and watching the gray and scarlet figure pass with its blooming cheeks, bright eyes, and elastic step. Having nothing else to 40 do, he took to petting this new whim, and quite depended on the daily stirring-up which the sight of the energetic damsel gave him. Kate saw it all, but took no notice. She was as soft as a summer sea, and by some clever stroke had Belle Morgan to tea that very week.

For the first time in his life, the "Crusher," as his male friends called him, got 45 crushed; for Belle, with the subtle skill of a quick-witted, keen-sighted girl, soon saw and condemned the elegant affectations which others called foreign polish.

311. Which of the following most accurately describes the purpose of the first paragraph?

(A) To mollify the reader before exploring some uncomfortable subjects
(B) To describe in detail the type of world that Belle Morgan stepped into
(C) To emphasize the differences between Kate and Belle
(D) To imply that the town had been brought to life by Lennox's presence
(E) To illustrate how poor and decrepit the town was

312. As used in line 4, the word "supercilious" most nearly means

(A) humble
(B) pompous
(C) diplomatic
(D) implacable
(E) endemic

313. In line 7, the expression "our first families" is analogous to

(A) the British colonists of the Americas
(B) the Norman invaders of Britain
(C) German Hessian soldiers in America
(D) the noble families from Spain in the Americas
(E) the descendants of Adam and Eve

314. As used in line 7, the word "decorous" most nearly means

(A) mendacious
(B) ferocious
(C) inexhaustible
(D) tenuous
(E) well-behaved

315. The narrator uses the clause "ennui claimed him for its own" to mean that

(A) Lennox was immensely bored by the end of the first week
(B) Lennox and Kate had gone on a vacation together
(C) Kate and Belle were both trying to marry Lennox
(D) Belle was Lennox's new guardian
(E) Lennox had forgotten his luggage at the train station

316. It can be inferred from the passage that

    (A) Lennox and Belle were brother and sister
    (B) Kate and Belle had been best friends since childhood
    (C) Belle and Lennox met previously during the summertime
    (D) Belle was the girl in the scarlet stockings
    (E) Kate and Lennox went to the same school in Boston

317. As used in line 10, the word "irradicable" most nearly means

    (A) assiduous
    (B) entrenched
    (C) saccharine
    (D) untoward
    (E) ephemeral

318. According to the passage, Belle can be described by all of the following words EXCEPT

    (A) blithe
    (B) wholesome
    (C) pleasant
    (D) lovable
    (E) meager

319. According to lines 27–30, which of the following statements best describes Belle's effect on people in the street?

    (A) She angered the high-society ladies, who saw her as impertinent.
    (B) She confused the citizens, who thought she was a ghost.
    (C) She exemplified all of the attributes that made the town so dull.
    (D) She enchanted and delighted everyone she passed.
    (E) She repulsed everyone, because she looked like an ogre.

320. As used in line 40, the word "elastic" most nearly means

    (A) accusatory
    (B) flexible
    (C) sedentary
    (D) quotidian
    (E) florid

321. In lines 36–38, the author suggests that Belle's presence

(A) has no effect on anyone in the town
(B) must come to an end soon
(C) has been detrimental to Kate
(D) is a complete contrast to her surroundings
(E) must remain a secret

322. Which of the following statements best describe(s) the reason why the narrator calls Belle a "a busy, bustling little body" in line 25?

   I. She was walking briskly to an unknown destination.
  II. Her clothes implied that she was a nurse.
 III. Her hands and pockets were full of packages.

(A) I
(B) I and II
(C) III
(D) I and III
(E) II and III

323. In lines 38–42, the narrator suggests that

(A) Belle gets out of school every day at 3 PM
(B) Kate is jealous of Belle's rosy complexion
(C) Lennox watches Belle pass by his window every day at 3 PM
(D) Belle is a dancer in the local ballet company
(E) Lennox cooks a pot of stew for lunch every day

324. It can be inferred from the last paragraph that

(A) Kate and Belle had become mortal enemies over their affections for Lennox
(B) when he was in Europe, Lennox was a championship bodybuilder
(C) Lennox was usually the heartbreaker, but this time a girl had caught his heart
(D) Belle was immediately accepted by the town's society
(E) Belle was from Europe, which immediately made her more attractive to Lennox

325. As used in line 47, the word "affectations" most nearly means

(A) derivatives
(B) abhorrence
(C) rejuvenation
(D) mannerisms
(E) disillusions

Passage 1

The assemblage of Egyptian antiquities in the British Museum in London is the world's largest and most comprehensive outside of Egypt. In existence since the museum's founding in 1753, the collection has grown to enormous proportions.

One of the greatest periods of expansion took place in the early nineteenth century. Napoleon's forces had invaded the region, intending to make it a stepstone 5
in the conquest of British India. However, the French forces were defeated in the Battle of the Nile. All of the Egyptian antiquities that had been acquired by the French were commandeered by the British army and offered to the British Museum in 1803. Among the many works taken at that time was the legendary Rosetta Stone, which made possible our modern understanding of Egyptian hieroglyphs. 10

Subsequently, the British Museum actively supported excavations in Egypt into the twentieth century. By 1924, the collection contained more than 50,000 objects. The museum gained hundreds more acquisitions until changes were made to antiquities laws in Egypt. In the 2000s alone, 12 million items were given to the British Museum's Egyptian collections by benefactors from around the world. 15

Some nations protest that so many cultural artifacts are housed outside of Egypt's borders. However, the fact remains that many of these objects would have been lost or destroyed hundreds of years ago had they not been placed in the British Museum's collection. The relics of the past belong to humanity, not just to nation-states, and they should be shared by all, and for all. 20

Passage 2

As shocking as it may seem, the shameful ownership of ill-gotten antiquities has continued unabated around the world for much of recent history, despite a number of laws and international agreements that came into force in the last century. As early as the turn of the twentieth century, nations around the world began to make it official government policy that all cultural property belongs to the 25
country, not to an excavator or buyer.

At present, the United Nations Educational, Scientific and Cultural Organization (UNESCO) 1970 Convention on the Means of Prohibiting the Illicit Import, Export and Transfer of Ownership of Cultural Property is the world's most influential and vigorous international antiquities agreement. The nations that signed 30
the agreement and became members of the convention are allowed to repossess stolen or illegally exported antiquities from other member states. Sadly, not all nations joined the convention immediately. For example, the United States did not incorporate the agreement into American law until 1983 and Britain did not become a signatory nation until 2001. 35

While it is important for nations of the world to carefully preserve and share their cultural history with other nations—and institutions such as museums, auction houses, and art galleries have been essential tools in that endeavor—each nation that has had antiquities pilfered from them for centuries should have the right to reclaim those items. The only solution is to share the artifacts through 40
traveling exhibitions, with the explicit understanding that they are simply on loan.

326. The authors of both passages describe

(A) the acquisition of antiquities
(B) the UNESCO convention
(C) the British Museum
(D) Egyptian pyramids
(E) the Battle of the Nile

327. As used in line 8 of Passage 1, the word "commandeered" most nearly means

(A) seized
(B) beset
(C) infuriated
(D) reproached
(E) quelled

328. The author's attitude in Passage 2 can best be described as

(A) evanescent
(B) vivacious
(C) foppish
(D) valorous
(E) outraged

329. It can be inferred from lines 14–15 of Passage 1 that

(A) the British Museum has given away more than 12 million items in the 2000s alone
(B) the Egyptian government is the new benefactor of the British Museum
(C) millions of objects have also been donated to the museum's Egyptian collections
(D) the British Museum's collection today contains only 50,000 objects
(E) all items donated to the British Museum have been returned to the Egyptian government

330. Which of the following statements best describes the changes mentioned in lines 13–14 of Passage 1?

(A) The British Museum actively supported excavations in the twentieth century.

(B) Antiquities laws in Egypt were modified to prohibit foreigners from funding and conducting excavations.

(C) The UNESCO convention is the world's most influential and vigorous international antiquities agreement.

(D) Napoleon's forces suffered a tremendous defeat in Egypt at the hands of the British.

(E) The Rosetta Stone is the most important ancient artifact ever found.

331. The author's primary purpose in writing Passage 2 is to

(A) recommend new amendments to the UNESCO convention

(B) explain the lack of Egyptian antiquities in the United States

(C) protest the involvement of the United Nations in antiquities issues

(D) criticize the continued ownership of stolen antiquities

(E) emphasize the benefits of museum collections

332. According to Passage 1, which of the following statements is NOT true about the British Museum?

(A) The museum's Egyptian collections have been sequestered by the Egyptian government.

(B) The museum has held the Rosetta Stone since 1803.

(C) The museum has more than 12 million objects in its Egyptian collections.

(D) The museum was founded in 1753.

(E) The museum has the largest collection of Egyptian artifacts outside of Cairo.

333. Which of the following statements is NOT supported by the second paragraph of Passage 2 (lines 27–35)?

(A) It took years for a number of nations to finally become members of the UNESCO convention.

(B) Britain did not join the UNESCO Convention until the twenty-first century.

(C) The UNESCO convention became U.S. law through the Convention on Cultural Property Implementation Act.

(D) UNESCO members can recuperate antiquities from other member states.

(E) The UNESCO convention is a robust international agreement regarding antiquities.

334. Which of the following statements most accurately describes the relationship between Passage 1 and Passage 2?
    (A) Passage 1 is a direct rebuttal of the ideas in Passage 2.
    (B) Both passages arrive at the same conclusion through different analyses.
    (C) Passage 1 provides an alternative theory to that of Passage 2.
    (D) The passages discuss the same topics, but they focus on different aspects of the topics.
    (E) Passage 2 provides the evidence to support the conclusions in Passage 1.

335. As used in line 39 of Passage 2, the word "pilfered" most nearly means
    (A) berated
    (B) repulse
    (C) curtailed
    (D) stolen
    (E) refuted

336. Which one of the following statements can be inferred from Passage 1?
    (A) Changes in Egyptian antiquities laws meant that finds from excavations were legalized.
    (B) The antiquities laws in Egypt were updated after a long, drawn-out battle between the national government of Egypt and collectors in foreign countries.
    (C) The Turkish National Museum has an impressive collection of antiquities.
    (D) The Rosetta Stone was the most important Egyptian artifact ever recovered.
    (E) The Egyptian galleries can display only a minuscule percentage of the British Museum's Egyptian holdings.

337. As used in line 22 of Passage 2, the word "unabated" most nearly means
    (A) unsubstantiated
    (B) subsided
    (C) unhindered
    (D) contaminated
    (E) expedited

When Silas Marner's sensibility returned, he continued the action which had been arrested, and closed his door, unaware of the chasm in his consciousness, unaware of any intermediate change, except that the light had grown dim, and that he was chilled and faint.

He thought he had been too long standing at the door and looking out. Turn- 5 ing towards the hearth, where the two logs had fallen apart, and sent forth only a red uncertain glimmer, he seated himself on his fireside chair, and was stooping to push his logs together, when, to his blurred vision, it seemed as if there were gold on the floor in front of the hearth.

Gold!—his own gold—brought back to him as mysteriously as it had been 10 taken away! He felt his heart begin to beat violently, and for a few moments he was unable to stretch out his hand and grasp the restored treasure. The heap of gold seemed to glow and get larger beneath his agitated gaze. He leaned forward at last, and stretched forth his hand; but instead of the hard coin with the familiar resist- ing outline, his fingers encountered soft warm curls. In utter amazement, Silas fell 15 on his knees and bent his head low to examine the marvel: it was a sleeping child— a round, fair thing, with soft yellow rings all over its head.

Could this be his little sister come back to him in a dream—his little sister whom he had carried about in his arms for a year before she died, when he was a small boy without shoes or stockings? That was the first thought that darted across 20 Silas's blank wonderment. Was it a dream?

He rose to his feet again, pushed his logs together, and, throwing on some dried leaves and sticks, raised a flame; but the flame did not disperse the vision—it only lit up more distinctly the little round form of the child, and its shabby cloth- ing. It was very much like his little sister. Silas sank into his chair powerless, under 25 the double presence of an inexplicable surprise and a hurrying influx of memories. How and when had the child come in without his knowledge? He had never been beyond the door.

But along with that question, and almost thrusting it away, there was a vision of the old home and the old streets leading to Lantern Yard—and within that 30 vision another, of the thoughts which had been present with him in those far-off scenes. The thoughts were strange to him now, like old friendships impossible to revive; and yet he had a dreamy feeling that this child was somehow a message come to him from that far-off life: it stirred fibres that had never been moved in years—old quiverings of tenderness—old impressions of awe at the presentiment 35 of some Power presiding over his life; for his imagination had not yet extricated itself from the sense of mystery in the child's sudden presence, and had formed no conjectures of ordinary natural means by which the event could have been brought about.

338. As used in line 1, the word "sensibility" most nearly means

(A) drudgery
(B) consciousness
(C) grandiloquence
(D) uproar
(E) cacophony

339. By which of the following statements can the action of the first paragraph be summarized?

(A) While standing at the door, some thieves knocked Marner out and stole his gold.
(B) After years in a coma, Marner woke up to find that his sister was no longer living in their childhood home.
(C) Years passed before Marner was able to go to a doctor to learn the cause of his frequent fainting spells.
(D) The door to Marner's home opened suddenly, and when he went to close it, he was knocked unconscious.
(E) When Marner regained consciousness, he assumed that he had passed out while closing the door, and he became aware that some time had passed.

340. Which of the following statements best describes the events in the second paragraph (lines 5–9)?

(A) In a daze, Marner mistook the baby's blond hair for the gold that had been stolen from him.
(B) Marner was in debt to a loan shark and realized he would need to give up the baby as collateral.
(C) After years of saving money, he was finally able to adopt a baby girl.
(D) The baby had been lost in the snow outside and came into the home seeking warmth.
(E) Marner's little sister was trying to hide the baby she had out of wedlock.

341. As used in line 13, the word "agitated" most nearly means

(A) quixotic
(B) disconcerted
(C) unctuous
(D) salient
(E) impertinent

342. According to lines 18–20, Marner at first assumed that he

   (A) had died and gone to heaven, where he was reunited with his sister

   (B) was experiencing a hallucinogenic effect of the medicine he was taking

   (C) was dreaming of his sister, who had passed away when they were children

   (D) had found the neighborhood child who had gone missing

   (E) was the victim of an elaborate prank

343. According to lines 22–25, when Marner managed to get the fire going, he expected the child

   (A) to run out screaming

   (B) to jump into the flames

   (C) to start to cry

   (D) to call the cops

   (E) to disappear

344. Which of the following statements is supported by the passage?

   (A) Marner was an ogre, living alone under a bridge near London.

   (B) The gold that was taken from Marner was used to help the child's mother.

   (C) The child's presence was a distraction to help the thieves steal the gold.

   (D) Marner had not thought about his happy childhood in a very long time.

   (E) Marner was an invalid, and the whole scene next to the fire was a dream.

345. In lines 32–33, Marner's sudden rush of memories were like

   (A) comforting and familiar games he played as a child

   (B) long-ago friendships that seem lost forever

   (C) mysterious echoes of a forgotten past

   (D) elegant strains of a lovely song

   (E) the violent crashing of a drum

346. Which of the following statements can be inferred from the passage about the child's role in Marner's life?

   (A) The child had replaced Marner's lost gold and was his life's new treasure.

   (B) The gold was not in fact stolen but was used to buy the child illegally.

   (C) The child was the daughter of his long-lost sister.

   (D) Marner was repulsed by her presence and wanted to see her gone.

   (E) The thieves who stole his gold had taken her hostage, then left her there.

La bohème is an opera in four acts, composed by Giacomo Puccini to an Italian libretto by Luigi Illica and Giuseppe Giacosa. It is based on *Scènes de la vie de bohème* by Henri Murger, a collection of vignettes portraying young bohemians living in the Latin Quarter of Paris in the 1840s.

The story follows the complicated and passionate relationships of the four 5 main characters, all of whom are young and desperately poor. Marcello is in love with the beautiful Musetta, who seeks a wealthy benefactor to get her out of her squalor. But the most famous story arc is that of the romance between Marcello's roommate, Rodolfo, who is a poet, and Mimi, who makes a living doing embroidery; their love comes to a tragic end. 10

The world premiere performance of *La bohème* took place at the Teatro Regio in Turin, Italy, in February 1896; it was conducted by the young Arturo Toscanini, who later rose to international prominence. The opera quickly became popular throughout Italy, and productions were soon mounted by companies in other Italian cities. 15

The first performance of *La bohème* outside Italy was at the Teatro Colón in Buenos Aires, Argentina, in June 1896. The opera became an immediate international phenomenon.

Even into the twenty-first century, artists have continued to perform the stirring opera. And numerous adaptations and derivative works have been created in 20 the decades since its premiere, most notably the Broadway musical *Rent*, which also became a major motion picture.

347. All of the following are true about *La bohème* EXCEPT

(A) It is written in French.
(B) The opera is set in Paris.
(C) There is a tragic love story.
(D) It became a huge success.
(E) The first performance was in Italy.

348. A "collection of vignettes" (line 3) is

(A) a gathering of antiques
(B) an assortment of foods
(C) an album of hits
(D) an anthology of stories
(E) a compilation of records

349. In lines 16–18, the author implies that

(A) *La bohème* has never been performed outside of Italy
(B) *La bohème*'s score is the most complicated in all of Italian opera
(C) *La bohème* is the world's most popular opera
(D) *La bohème* can only be performed by Italian citizens
(E) the opera has been performed in countries around the world

350. With which of the following statements would the author most likely agree?

(A) *La bohème* has an enduring likability and will be loved, in various forms, by many generations.
(B) *La bohème* is completely overrated and should stop being performed.
(C) The Italian libretto was originally written by two German poets.
(D) *La bohème* may be the most expensive opera performed at the Teatro Colón.
(E) Arturo Toscanini was already world-famous by the time he conducted *La bohème*.

PART 2

SAT Sentence Completion

CHAPTER 5

Set 1: Low-Difficulty Questions

351. Angela thought her assignment overseas would be an exciting adventure, but in reality, it turned out to be a(n) _____ office job.

(A) prosaic
(B) amicable
(C) elaborate
(D) boisterous
(E) vivacious

352. The _____ student was class president, graduated at the top of her class, and was a member of the varsity volleyball team.

(A) capacious
(B) verbose
(C) dubious
(D) assiduous
(E) heinous

353. It was _____ that her sister was able to babysit, or else Janie would not have been able to make it to the crucial dress rehearsal tonight.

(A) egregious
(B) fortuitous
(C) mundane
(D) impeccable
(E) verdant

354. Since the insult I _____ to Shannon was not in fact her fault, she and I are able to come to a(n) _____.

(A) aspired . . precipice
(B) goaded . . trepidation
(C) imputed . . reconciliation
(D) exhorted . . hiatus
(E) perused . . aspersion

355. The only way the young artist was able to survive in a city as expensive as New York City on her _____ part-time salary at the corner deli was by being _____.

(A) illicit . . garrulous
(B) pervasive . . deliberate
(C) accessible . . bombastic
(D) meager . . frugal
(E) figurative . . hapless

356. I thought that the new novel by Madeleine LeCroix would be original and exhilarating, but I found the plot to be _____ and dull.

(A) harrowing
(B) fervent
(C) insolent
(D) saccharine
(E) hackneyed

357. The _____ old man yelled angrily at Billy when he accidentally threw a baseball over the fence.

(A) submissive
(B) transient
(C) rancorous
(D) condescending
(E) flabbergasted

358. I could see the look of growing _____ on the saleswoman's face as she continued in her attempt to appease the irate customer.

(A) exasperation
(B) accommodation
(C) duplicitous
(D) forbearance
(E) commendation

359. I tuned in to the debate to learn more about the candidate's economic policies, but he kept _____ with stories about his family and upbringing.

(A) innovating
(B) emulating
(C) digressing
(D) consigning
(E) insinuating

360. Your _____ solution to the complicated problem between these freshman roommates was incredibly helpful.

(A) sagacious
(B) insatiable
(C) cordial
(D) bashful
(E) primeval

361. Everyone thinks I am to blame, but when I prove that Claire was the one who stole the cookies from the office refrigerator, I will be _____.

(A) berated
(B) censured
(C) reproached
(D) quelled
(E) vindicated

362. Emily's family is so wealthy and fashionable, no matter how much he may desire to be like them, there is no way Derek will be able to _____ their _____ lifestyle using his cashier's salary.

(A) repulse . . corrosive
(B) curtail . . extraneous
(C) deface . . deleterious
(D) emulate . . opulent
(E) refute . . quotidian

363. Despite his intense nervousness around her, Harry attempted to be _____ when he spoke to Amy.

(A) nonchalant
(B) sedentary
(C) resilient
(D) acerbic
(E) ephemeral

364. Although you are furious with Shayna, because her gossiping almost got you in trouble with the boss, I recommend that you calm down and take a(n) _____ approach to your conversation with her.
- (A) accusatory
- (B) frigid
- (C) untoward
- (D) lewd
- (E) prudent

365. They said that he was a brilliant orator, but I found the language of his speech to be too _____, because it was overwrought and long-winded.
- (A) amorous
- (B) florid
- (C) meager
- (D) pugnacious
- (E) depraved

366. Carrie is a huge asset to our group, a(n) _____ employee, with her _____ work ethic and positive attitude.
- (A) profane . . querulous
- (B) adamant . . sophomoric
- (C) impassive . . stoic
- (D) taciturn . . perfidious
- (E) exemplary . . diligent

367. Although artist Vincent van Gogh and author Edgar Allan Poe might have felt _____ during their lifetimes, their work is now considered to be quite influential.
- (A) pretentious
- (B) whimsical
- (C) recalcitrant
- (D) facile
- (E) inconsequential

368. Mr. Jones, a _____ statesman, was stationed in the Pacific theater during World War II and was a successful businessman before serving in the state senate for more than fifteen years.

(A) felicitous
(B) latent
(C) petulant
(D) venerable
(E) insipid

369. Although President Truman disliked Stalin and was _____ him, the U.S. president had to _____ with him because Russia was also a member of the Allied forces.

(A) fond of . . defile
(B) wary of . . collaborate
(C) deferential to . . nurture
(D) accommodating to . . elude
(E) scared of . . chastise

370. Brenda hoped that her current success was not _____, since it had been a dream of hers since childhood to be a pop music icon.

(A) derivative
(B) placid
(C) ephemeral
(D) variegated
(E) contemporaneous

371. The dishonest mayor attempted to _____ her opponent in the campaign by running _____ ads in the local newspapers.

(A) discredit . . libelous
(B) venerate . . docile
(C) console . . contrite
(D) infuriate . . pellucid
(E) appease . . slanderous

372. The _____ of the CEO's impressive career can be credited to her ability to adapt to new circumstances and to seize new opportunities while climbing the corporate ladder.

(A) domesticity
(B) longevity
(C) resonance
(D) cacophony
(E) protuberance

373. John D. Rockefeller was a _____ businessman who pored over every possible aspect of his company in order to cut costs and increase profits.

(A) quixotic
(B) vindictive
(C) diabolic
(D) meticulous
(E) devious

374. After learning of all the incredible obstacles she had overcome to make it to the audition, it was evident to the show's producers that Marie had a(n) _____ desire to become a successful actress.

(A) devious
(B) tenacious
(C) congenial
(D) promiscuous
(E) irascible

375. Romeo made the tragic and _____ decision to kill himself before he could find out the truth about Juliet from his friend the friar.

(A) lackadaisical
(B) opulent
(C) aboriginal
(D) malevolent
(E) impetuous

376. Although the two coworkers seemed to be always at odds, their relationship was actually quite _____.

(A) maudlin
(B) amicable
(C) rustic
(D) tortuous
(E) caustic

377. Mary and Sam did not agree on the extent to which harmful greenhouse gases have a(n) _____ effect on the environment, leading them to have a(n) _____ discussion.

(A) invulnerable . . outrageous
(B) audacious . . pecuniary
(C) deleterious . . querulous
(D) convivial . . superlative
(E) eminent . . malleable

378. The loud and rowdy children on the field trip did not show the appropriate _____ while visiting Arlington Cemetery.

(A) modernity
(B) diversity
(C) guile
(D) abhorrence
(E) reverence

379. The wound that killed the general appeared to be _____ and harmless; we did not learn until much later that it was deep and had punctured several vital organs.

(A) abnormal
(B) carnivorous
(C) gratuitous
(D) mediocre
(E) superficial

380. In the 1960s, thousands of people fled Cuba after Fidel Castro took power, seeking political _____ in the United States and other countries.

(A) asylum
(B) meditation
(C) rejuvenation
(D) egotism
(E) urgency

381. Connor attempted to hide his _____ for his daughter's new boyfriend, Aaron, but his _____ remarks and mean-spirited scoffing made it obvious.

(A) disdain . . condescending
(B) irrelevance . . eligible
(C) patriotism . . socialist
(D) avarice . . casual
(E) remission . . eloquent

382. The reporters were not allowed to ask the politician about the _____ photos published in the tabloids of him being handcuffed by police outside a Las Vegas casino.

(A) banal
(B) provocative
(C) foppish
(D) mercenary
(E) vacuous

383. Her bouffant hairdo and poodle skirt were _____; she looked out of place at the punk rock concert.

(A) evanescent
(B) anachronistic
(C) valorous
(D) litigious
(E) neutral

384. The police were called to the high school football game, as a _____ of disorderly fans from the rival teams resulted in violent fights.

(A) nomination
(B) addendum
(C) convergence
(D) prominence
(E) mockery

385. With his late-night parties and wild spending sprees, it was only a matter of time before Andrew's _____ behavior landed him in jail or cost him his job.

(A) motley
(B) nautical
(C) hedonistic
(D) resilient
(E) benign

386. Sara was unable to _____ the _____ she felt after winning the game and began to do a victory dance, despite being told not to by her coach.

(A) beset . . extortion
(B) suppress . . jubilation
(C) mesmerize . . telepathy
(D) wrangle . . appellation
(E) tantalize . . disillusion

387. "The _____ of this nation depends on our ability to educate our citizens and to create jobs, so Americans can once again be on the road to financial success," the politician said in his speech.

(A) prosperity
(B) dispensation
(C) adjuration
(D) remission
(E) upheaval

388. It is past my curfew, so I need to enter the house _____ in order to avoid detection.

(A) vivaciously
(B) surreptitiously
(C) absurdly
(D) chaotically
(E) ignominiously

389. With just two weeks on the job, John was a(n) _____, but his enthusiasm made up for his lack of experience.

(A) imitator
(B) scholar
(C) arbiter
(D) novice
(E) tyrant

390. I did not study until the night before and got a terrible grade on that test, but that was the _____ conclusion of my _____.

(A) inevitable . . procrastination
(B) scrupulous . . absolution
(C) encyclical . . obsolescence
(D) ligneous . . intolerance
(E) opportunistic . . intemperance

391. The difference between the paint swatches labeled "off-white" and "cream" was too _____ for Fabian to detect.

(A) passive
(B) acetic
(C) garrulous
(D) dilatory
(E) subtle

392. The interior designer's colorful aesthetic was clearly a(n) _____ talent, as she had no formal education or training before creating her successful business.

(A) equestrian
(B) jocular
(C) momentary
(D) intuitive
(E) counterfeit

393. The _____ feelings of patriotic camaraderie disappeared a few months after the terrorist attacks.

(A) acrimonious
(B) venerable
(C) transient
(D) paternal
(E) formidable

394. The _____ certainly made some rousing speeches, but he proved to have a flimsy platform and no solutions when tested at the electoral debates.

(A) freemason
(B) .gendarme
(C) harbinger
(D) demagogue
(E) prodigy

395. Henry VIII was such a paranoid leader that he thought anyone who disagreed with him was _____, and he never allowed anyone to _____ his position of power.

(A) unctuous . . entrench
(B) perfidious . . usurp
(C) cadaverous . . exacerbate
(D) altruistic . . outride
(E) enthusiastic . . satirize

396. Janelle could not be counted on to be _____, as she was always insensitive to other people's feelings and indiscreet about personal information.

(A) sanctimonious
(B) vapid
(C) whimsical
(D) frivolous
(E) tactful

397. The architecture of the Baroque period, with its gold-leaf ornamentation and opulent use of color, is considered by many to be among the most _____.

(A) tactful
(B) furtive
(C) conducive
(D) judicious
(E) ostentatious

398. I will be moving soon into a smaller house to save money, so I will have to have a garage sale to sell any _____ items.

(A) superfluous
(B) lackadaisical
(C) ravenous
(D) versatile
(E) callow

399. Despite his disagreeable run-in with the homeless lady, Derek felt _____ for her sad situation.

(A) compassion
(B) calumny
(C) abhorrence
(D) redundancy
(E) disinterest

400. The hate speech that the gentleman began to express at our church meeting was met with boos and he was asked to leave, since it was _____ with the open and accepting nature of our congregation.

(A) remonstrant
(B) correlative
(C) incompatible
(D) exhaustive
(E) onerous

CHAPTER 6

Set 2: Medium-Difficulty Questions

401. Miranda considered it a matter of _____ to defend her classmate who was being taunted by the bully, even though she was just as scared.

(A) abeyance
(B) integrity
(C) termination
(D) redolence
(E) extravagance

402. The friendship of a studious and _____ boy like Cliff will be a good influence on my _____ and disrespectful nephew.

(A) factious . . observant
(B) bountiful . . statuesque
(C) intolerant . . frolicsome
(D) vulgar . . baritone
(E) benevolent . . enervating

403. The Texans in the Alamo were unwilling to _____ with or surrender to Mexican General Santa Anna, and they paid the ultimate price.

(A) compromise
(B) bedeck
(C) ostracize
(D) vegetate
(E) convulse

404. I am not _____: I would much rather drive my dad's vintage Volkswagen Beetle than be seen in my sister's flashy new sports car.

(A) disreputable
(B) fugacious
(C) pretentious
(D) impervious
(E) rampant

405. Roald Amundsen was a(n) _____ explorer; he was the first person to visit both the North and South poles.

(A) abrupt
(B) pugnacious
(C) tranquil
(D) generic
(E) intrepid

406. Every minute of Lara's life was scheduled and carefully planned, leaving no room for fun or _____.

(A) spontaneity
(B) grievance
(C) persecution
(D) absolution
(E) severance

407. Because of the threats against witnesses by gangs in the neighborhood, the best the police could hope for was to receive _____ tips about the brazen shooting.

(A) versatile
(B) palatial
(C) brittle
(D) expressive
(E) anonymous

408. I asked Ellen many intimate questions about my relationship with deceased relatives to see if she could _____ her claim that she is clairvoyant.

(A) contaminate
(B) substantiate
(C) percolate
(D) deluge
(E) stifle

409. I was amazed at how _____ the mother was in the courtroom, considering the fact that she was looking into the eyes of her daughter's killer; I could not have had the same remarkable self-control.

(A) restrained
(B) studious
(C) astute
(D) livid
(E) expeditious

410. I did not believe that Madelyn was a _____ child until I heard her play the Mozart concerto.

(A) litigious
(B) subservient
(C) precocious
(D) coercive
(E) mediocre

411. The detective _____ every piece of information in the cold case file in an attempt to find new leads.

(A) scrutinized
(B) abominated
(C) deteriorated
(D) refracted
(E) transfused

412. None of what Katherine said about me is true, and I will confront her about making those _____ remarks.

(A) tranquil
(B) spurious
(C) penitential
(D) circuitous
(E) tireless

413. We have such _____ ideas about how to approach economic policy that I don't know how we will ever come to an agreement.

(A) mundane
(B) divergent
(C) negligent
(D) acoustic
(E) conformist

414. The _____ of the sixteenth-century church was expensive and time-consuming, but the visitors all agreed that it was remarkable to see the building restored to its former glory.

(A) obstruction
(B) capitulation
(C) renovation
(D) jurisdiction
(E) malediction

415. I hope that there are _____ circumstances to justify your arriving home past curfew.

(A) meticulous
(B) translucent
(C) voracious
(D) deplorable
(E) extenuating

416. Eric's ability to avoid jail time is _____ upon his performing 1,000 hours of community service.

(A) devious
(B) nocturnal
(C) ambidextrous
(D) irritable
(E) conditional

417. It seems impossible after our decades-long friendship, but our former _____ has disappeared completely because of your betrayal.

(A) camaraderie
(B) nomination
(C) rebelliousness
(D) intrusion
(E) subsistence

418. The teacher said that Iago was the _____ in Shakespeare's famous play, but I felt that Othello was not exactly the hero of the story, as he also acted cruelly and selfishly.

(A) journalist
(B) matron
(C) laureate
(D) recluse
(E) antagonist

419. Gwendolyn did not apologize because she cares about Stacy's feelings; she only acted in a(n) _____ way to avoid _____ from her peers, who said she had behaved poorly.

(A) diligent . . lunacy
(B) exemplary . . pantomime
(C) accessible . . mutiny
(D) contrite . . censure
(E) logical . . martyrdom

420. Because Carol was deathly allergic to peanuts, she was forced to _____ from eating many of the treats at Dustin's birthday party.

(A) paralyze
(B) interrogate
(C) castigate
(D) abstain
(E) dilate

421. In this age of viral videos and social media, fame comes quickly, but it is also _____, since people swiftly move on to the next fad.

(A) intracellular
(B) laborious
(C) pastoral
(D) evanescent
(E) redolent

422. The defense lawyer knew that the evidence against his client was unfavorable, so he would have to depend on _____ from the jury to gain _____ for his client.

(A) reminiscence . . turpitude
(B) urgency . . venom
(C) empathy . . leniency
(D) courtesy . . repentance
(E) cynicism . . deformity

423. She was once a(n) _____ person, but she became angry and _____ after the car accident left her paralyzed and scarred.

(A) effervescent . . reclusive
(B) degenerate . . nonpareil
(C) doleful . . obnoxious
(D) expeditious . . rigorous
(E) munificent . . perspicacious

424. The scientist worked around the clock to find an antibiotic that could eliminate this deadly, _____ strain of bacteria.

(A) ribald
(B) seditious
(C) ignoble
(D) docile
(E) virulent

425. After taking the three-hour tour of the Grand Canyon on foot, the kids and I fell in love with the _____ but beautiful landscape of the Arizona desert.

(A) parched
(B) resilient
(C) ecstatic
(D) inquisitive
(E) furtive

426. Your _____ explanation is making it hard for me to focus and fully understand the complicated physics problem you are talking about.

(A) orthodox
(B) circuitous
(C) averse
(D) inseparable
(E) prominent

427. Eddie's _____ for the band was obvious; not only did he own every album, but he also collected Beatles memorabilia and studio-session recordings.

(A) aversion
(B) coalescence
(C) reverence
(D) dismissal
(E) insomnia

428. Researchers are working diligently on ways to _____ the picture quality of the old films, which have become faded with age.

(A) invert
(B) enhance
(C) paralyze
(D) abase
(E) reprimand

429. We all gathered around to hear Uncle Clark's and Aunt Sue's
_____ of their trip to Tierra del Fuego and Antarctica.

(A) theology
(B) variance
(C) entrails
(D) jargon
(E) anecdotes

430. It is going to take a great deal of _____ to get Harriet's CD back;
Carrie will have to sneak into the room when her sister is not around and
avoid moving her things out of place.

(A) kinship
(B) legerdemain
(C) bulwark
(D) suffrage
(E) needlework

431. The _____ of my argument is simple: I could not have been at the
bar when you said I was, since I was in the library studying, and Mary can
back me up on that claim.

(A) dissertation
(B) brimstone
(C) linchpin
(D) paradox
(E) memento

432. The criminal's _____ for finely tailored suits was his downfall;
he wore them so often that it was easy for witnesses to remember him
and point him out to the police.

(A) proclivity
(B) sarcasm
(C) gratuity
(D) denouement
(E) trepidation

433. Many people in this country feel that our legal system is bogged down by _____ lawsuits by people who are looking for money or fame, not for justice.

(A) delectable
(B) ungainly
(C) blithe
(D) chromatic
(E) frivolous

434. The woman's _____ about the dangers of kryptonite in the city's drinking water made it clear to police that she was not a credible witness.

(A) radiance
(B) harangue
(C) moratorium
(D) zephyr
(E) colloquialism

435. If Terrence had a(n) _____ of decency, he would have removed that _____ durian fruit from the room before the terrible odor made Maria gag.

(A) coincidence . . mandatory
(B) comparison . . misanthropic
(C) irritant . . equivalent
(D) modicum . . pungent
(E) macrocosm . . epizootic

436. She wore the most beautiful dress, made of a(n) _____ fabric that made her look as though she were dressed in sunlight.

(A) estimable
(B) antediluvian
(C) diaphanous
(D) vociferous
(E) philharmonic

437. There is a _____ relationship between the two brothers; they are just one small misunderstanding away from never speaking to each other again.

(A) tenuous
(B) phonetic
(C) nefarious
(D) bellicose
(E) fallacious

438. The laconic, timid girl was the exact opposite of her _____, extroverted mother.

(A) ferocious
(B) auriferous
(C) endemic
(D) pious
(E) garrulous

439. As we toured the streets of Paris, we were overwhelmed by the _____ of the architecture, especially the beautiful bridges along the Seine River.

(A) zenith
(B) pulchritude
(C) expulsion
(D) irreverence
(E) detriment

440. I grew tired of listening to the politician's _____ speeches about the importance of family, especially since I knew that she hadn't spoken to her mother in more than five years.

(A) sanctimonious
(B) desultory
(C) infrequent
(D) neglectful
(E) concurrent

441. We hold up historical figures like George Washington and Abraham Lincoln as _____ of American bravery and patriotism.

(A) nemesis
(B) typography
(C) vernacular
(D) paragons
(E) assessors

442. I was being _____ when I said I knew all about how to use the latest programs; I do not know anything about them, since I am in fact a _____ at graphic design.

(A) atrocious . . mendicant
(B) mendacious . . neophyte
(C) immaterial . . prospector
(D) diplomatic . . spinster
(E) audacious . . collier

443. Emily did not let me into her room, as she did not want me to laugh at her and _____ her obsession with My Little Pony dolls.

(A) carouse
(B) enshrine
(C) redress
(D) deride
(E) legislate

444. Contemporaries described Catherine the Great as _____; betray her once, and you lost her confidence forever.

(A) implacable
(B) minute
(C) reliant
(D) winsome
(E) granular

445. It was not my intention to _____ Sandra with my album choices for our road trip, as I could not imagine that someone could hate the Bee Gees so much.

(A) dispossess
(B) vex
(C) atone
(D) recede
(E) consecrate

446. Karen's accusations that I cheated to win the baking contest threaten to _____ my reputation as an honest competitor.

(A) rebuild
(B) underlie
(C) stimulate
(D) wrangle
(E) defile

447. Colin had reached the _____ of his career as a comedian when he could not even book a performance at amateur night in the sleazy Hoboken Club.

(A) zeitgeist
(B) epitome
(C) junction
(D) nadir
(E) omission

448. The buffet was _____ with dishes from around the world; it seemed as though every nation was represented with at least two examples of their local cuisine.

(A) replete
(B) inconceivable
(C) ghastly
(D) duteous
(E) inedible

449. Unfortunately for President Lincoln, General McClellan proved to be an ineffectual and _____ leader, unable to be decisive on the battlefield.

(A) inexhaustible
(B) populous
(C) capricious
(D) stupendous
(E) corpulent

450. My experience at the seminar was amazing; I learned a great deal and thoroughly enjoyed the intelligent _____ between the political science experts.

(A) hillock
(B) repartee
(C) grotto
(D) homonym
(E) cosmos

CHAPTER 7

Set 3: High-Difficulty Questions

451. After going to the annual quilt show, Nancy was overwhelmed by the
_____ of _____ fabrics and patterns to choose from
for her next project.

(A) surfeit . . multifarious
(B) abrasion . . outrageous
(C) circumference . . partisan
(D) drudgery . . rebellious
(E) omniscience . . boorish

452. Georgia told Melissa that she was never going to find a boyfriend
sufficiently _____ for her taste, since she demands
round-the-clock attention and constant compliments.

(A) botanical
(B) obsequious
(C) discernible
(D) spasmodic
(E) fictitious

453. At the gallery, we were delighted with the _____ of the
delicate, airy watercolor paintings and the bulky, ornate frames;
the contrast really made the artwork come alive.

(A) pyromania
(B) stoicism
(C) opulence
(D) locomotion
(E) juxtaposition

454. The CEO had to be fired, since the company could not defend his malicious _____ against their top rival, which was caught on tape and played endlessly on cable news.

(A) alienation
(B) palette
(C) invective
(D) forecast
(E) proctor

455. Our new, _____ supervisor is constantly reminding us about the company's dress code and the types of decorations that are allowed in employees' cubicles.

(A) punctilious
(B) munificent
(C) foreordained
(D) odoriferous
(E) surreptitious

456. We were forced to fire Todd because of his tardiness as well as the _____ jokes he would tell, despite being told that most people in the office found them offensive.

(A) susceptible
(B) inquisitive
(C) judicious
(D) ribald
(E) legible

457. Social media websites, while entertaining and a great way to bring people together, are _____; irresponsible posts can ruin your college and job prospects.

(A) legitimate
(B) plebeian
(C) sanctimonious
(D) cadaverous
(E) insidious

458. After receiving her master's degree in petroleum engineering, Carol has a(n) _____ of job options, as there are too few graduates to fill the many open positions out there.

(A) cacophony
(B) epiphany
(C) plethora
(D) bureaucracy
(E) iniquity

459. I am going to have my aunt read my college application essay, since she is intelligent and _____, making her the perfect proofreader.

(A) inimical
(B) mawkish
(C) supple
(D) fastidious
(E) profligate

460. The _____ with which Chuck called Melody after getting her phone number was not surprising, considering how beautiful she is and how enchanted he was by her at their first meeting.

(A) suspension
(B) tenet
(C) vivisection
(D) derision
(E) alacrity

461. The origin of the phrase "dressed to the nines" is unknown, but some historians _____ that it came from the amount of fabric needed to create an expensive, elegant garment.

(A) disavow
(B) surmise
(C) uproot
(D) protrude
(E) officiate

462. Selena does not realize that her _____ makes her arguments sound more condescending than _____.

(A) pyromania . . rabid
(B) qualm . . supine
(C) grandiloquence . . cogent
(D) zeal . . euphonious
(E) minion . . phlegmatic

463. The consumerism that drives people to live beyond their means is a(n)
_____ element of our society, driving individuals into the terrible
chasm of debts they cannot repay.

(A) acoustic
(B) momentary
(C) galvanic
(D) innocuous
(E) pernicious

464. Nancy could not be _____ into joining the Girl Scouts, even
though we pleaded endlessly and tried to tempt her with offers of free
cookies.

(A) insinuated
(B) requited
(C) augured
(D) cajoled
(E) preordained

465. Snow White was young, beautiful, and _____, which angered the
cruel and _____ queen, who chose to destroy her.

(A) winsome . . nefarious
(B) laconic . . productive
(C) puissant . . cosmetic
(D) artless . . convivial
(E) deceitful . . bombastic

466. Rebekah _____ between her suitors—the poor but loving Philip
and the cold but wealthy Charles—unable to make a choice.

(A) burnished
(B) vacillated
(C) gesticulated
(D) surmised
(E) lacerated

467. The period between 1945 and 1992 is known as the Cold War, because
the hostility between nations and the threat of nuclear destruction were
_____ a perilous physical, "hot" war fought with bombs and guns.

(A) transcendent of
(B) ascendant to
(C) exorbitant in
(D) inherent of
(E) tantamount to

468. According to the school principal, the local government's ideas about how to distribute this year's taxes are so _____ that they will only lead to confusion and a misuse of funds.

(A) ashen
(B) draconian
(C) vernal
(D) nimble
(E) obtuse

469. *Into the Wild* is a book about a regular man from a middle-class background who chose to _____ his _____ lifestyle in order to live in the Alaskan wilderness, with tragic consequences.

(A) animate . . unutterable
(B) connive . . angular
(C) purloin . . defensible
(D) eschew . . conventional
(E) decipher . . uproarious

470. I know that Jessica took my iPod charger without asking; her shuffling feet and shifty eyes _____ her guilt.

(A) arrogate
(B) evince
(C) repudiate
(D) proscribe
(E) reprove

471. I am going to have to _____ my offer to drive the carpool this week, since I will be out of town.

(A) abase
(B) preoccupy
(C) cull
(D) rescind
(E) deign

472. Janice stayed up all night studying, and try as she might with coffee and energy drinks, she could not shake that _____ feeling the next morning.

(A) somnolent
(B) quixotic
(C) inchoate
(D) effulgent
(E) scurrilous

473. The governor held a press conference to publicly admit his wrongdoing in an attempt to prove that he was _____.

(A) cursory
(B) execrable
(C) fecund
(D) contrite
(E) unctuous

474. The chief of police vowed to find the people who _____ the cemetery by spray-painting the mausoleums and knocking over tombstones.

(A) abrogated
(B) transmuted
(C) desecrated
(D) undulated
(E) dissembled

475. Emily had been doing so well in English class that I was shocked to find that her latest essay assignment was full of _____ errors and obvious mistakes.

(A) vacuous
(B) incontrovertible
(C) egregious
(D) perfunctory
(E) sacrosanct

476. The _____ criminal thought that he could make a clean getaway in the stolen car, but unfortunately for him, it was equipped with a GPS-enabled security system.

(A) salient
(B) feral
(C) discursive
(D) oblique
(E) hapless

477. Of course Lana took _____ at your comments; she thought she looked great, but you said her hairstyle and clothes were sad and old-fashioned.

(A) sagacity
(B) umbrage
(C) iniquity
(D) hegemony
(E) panacea

478. My aunt Martha says that my generation's youth is _____: we do not respect our elders and we do not know what "polite conversation" is.

(A) impertinent
(B) diffident
(C) providential
(D) voracious
(E) primeval

479. Tensions between the two nations escalated when the president made _____ comments about the other country at a meeting of the United Nations.

(A) propitious
(B) aerial
(C) vapid
(D) demure
(E) pejorative

480. After seeing the poor results of my annual physical, I had to hear my doctor once again _____ the health benefits of regular exercise and a sensible diet.

(A) adumbrate
(B) extol
(C) impinge
(D) dither
(E) rebuke

481. The tuberculosis left her _____ and weak, but she maintained her joyful, _____ view of life until the end.

(A) execrable . . pugnacious
(B) cursory . . restive
(C) pallid . . sanguine
(D) desiccated . . inimical
(E) ebullient . . fractious

482. When I see you hanging out in your room posting on Facebook, I _____ the premise that you cannot help your mother take out the trash.

(A) renounce
(B) enervate
(C) inveterate
(D) obfuscate
(E) decry

483. Clara was tired of her brother's teasing her that she had taken up a(n) _____ way of life, because she got rid of her Internet connection and gave up red meat.

(A) rife
(B) scurrilous
(C) tractable
(D) ascetic
(E) viscous

484. The look on my mother's face was essentially a(n) _____ refusal of my request to go to the party on the other side of town.

(A) tacit
(B) variegated
(C) exigent
(D) languid
(E) obstreperous

485. It is dangerous to _____ government policies in totalitarian regimes, since any criticism is often met with severe punishment.

(A) palliate
(B) rebuke
(C) decry
(D) venerate
(E) buffet

486. Harry is energetic and funny, but most people misinterpret his quiet voice and _____ responses as evidence that he's shy or awkward.

(A) impervious
(B) laconic
(C) obdurate
(D) laborious
(E) resurgent

487. My grandmother told wonderful stories about what it was like in New York City at the end of World War II, running in the streets among the _____ crowds.

(A) servile
(B) timorous
(C) ingenuous
(D) hostile
(E) jubilant

488. Florence Nightingale was brave and compassionate; she helped soldiers who had been wounded on remote, dangerous, _____ battlefields.

(A) limpid
(B) officious
(C) pellucid
(D) fetid
(E) maudlin

489. The Boy Scouts had been camping for five days to get a number of merit badges, so their pride and satisfaction with a wonderful experience was _____ with being happy to go home to a hot shower.

(A) delectable
(B) penurious
(C) concomitant
(D) solipsistic
(E) protean

490. Rupert's caustic, _____ personality makes him _____ to us; we try to avoid his company as much as we can.

(A) extant . . antidote
(B) myriad . . maelstrom
(C) mercurial . . anathema
(D) solicitous . . iconoclast
(E) ostensible . . platitude

491. When the socialite was denied entry to the invitation-only party, she began to pout and stomp her feet like a _____ child.

(A) spurious
(B) querulous
(C) torpid
(D) derelict
(E) supernumerary

492. The young man was _____ in his quest to get the job of his dreams; he worked hard at several internships and contacted a number of college alumni, requesting interviews.

(A) pertinacious
(B) torrid
(C) jocose
(D) exemplary
(E) ichthyic

493. From afar, Beatrice looked like a pleasant, kind-hearted grandmother, but in reality, she had a cold, _____ personality.

(A) vitriolic
(B) illusive
(C) moribund
(D) penurious
(E) impious

494. The opposing team was _____ in their defeat; they congratulated us, and even invited some of us to go get a bite to eat after the game.

(A) perennial
(B) magnanimous
(C) inglorious
(D) eccentric
(E) trenchant

495. "The hostile _____ that is this administration's foreign policy is going to lead to misunderstandings, which could culminate in our nation's going to war," said the politician on the cable network show.

(A) veracity
(B) serendipity
(C) morass
(D) probity
(E) pathos

496. Even though the teacher caught her red-handed, Shannon had the _____ to deny using her smartphone during last week's test to search for answers on the Internet.

(A) portent
(B) perspicacity
(C) munificence
(D) temerity
(E) credulity

497. Although Apple computers seem to have a(n) _____ presence in the marketplace, they only account for five percent of sales.

    (A) ineffable
    (B) ubiquitous
    (C) crustaceous
    (D) harmonious
    (E) noxious

498. The _____ produced by the stray cats in the neighborhood used to drive us crazy at night; it was impossible to get any sleep.

    (A) paucity
    (B) cacophony
    (C) effrontery
    (D) approbation
    (E) conflagration

499. It was oddly _____ that I chose to change my travel plans; I would have had to sit in my hotel room all week, because the hurricane made landfall the day after I was scheduled to arrive.

    (A) nugatory
    (B) oblong
    (C) palpable
    (D) redoubtable
    (E) prescient

500. The _____ of Lauren's high school experience was being both homecoming queen and class valedictorian.

    (A) acrimony
    (B) zenith
    (C) protrusion
    (D) homage
    (E) antipathy

ANSWERS

Chapter 1: Set 1 Questions

1. (D) Since the records were burned and destroyed in a fire, the word "consumed" most nearly means incinerated.

2. (B) Overall, the author believes that information and data from the past is very important from historical and cultural perspectives, among others. In fact, the applications of such information are stated to be "limitless." The author describes the records of the 1890 census as "inimitable," because they were unique and would have provided insights into nineteenth-century American life.

3. (E) The passage does not state that the 1890 census was printed in a number of languages.

4. (D) In this context, the word "vigilant" most nearly means attentive.

5. (E) The author's conclusion is that the government didn't become "vigilant and proactive about the safety and preservation of historical records" until the twentieth century, so the fact that a special building where archives could be properly stored was built in 1930 best supports that conclusion.

6. (E) Based on the passage, it is impossible to conclude that people living in cooler climates have less efficient body temperature controls than those who live in warmer climates.

7. (C) The author gives blinking and blood circulation as examples of involuntary processes. Breathing is the only answer choice that fits this description; the other choices are voluntary.

8. (D) The author mentions reptiles in order to contrast reptiles' way of handling temperature changes with the way mammals do.

9. (B) The "core" is most analogous to the body's center.

10. (C) In this context, the word "ambient" most nearly means surrounding, as in the room's temperature.

11. (D) The author's primary purpose is to argue for decreasing beef production in order to reduce pollution.

12. (B) The conclusion is flawed, because it doesn't consider other methods of reducing greenhouse gas emissions.

13. (B) In this context, the word "copious" most nearly means profuse.

14. (E) Statement II about methane is supported by the fourth paragraph, and statement III about deforestation is supported by the third paragraph.

15. (A) The author would most likely agree that beef production generates more greenhouse gases than production of any other food we consume. The author states in the second paragraph that plant-based food production has a "less intense" environmental impact.

16. (B) In this context, the word "detrimentally" most nearly means destructively.

17. (E) In the second paragraph, the author states that "grain crops that could be used for . . . renewable energy such as biofuels must be used to feed the cattle."

18. (B) In this context, the word "dire" most nearly means urgent.

19. (B) The primary purpose of the fifth paragraph is to explain the reasons behind the growing scale of the beef production industry, specifically the issues of supply and demand.

20. (C) In this context, the word "correlate" most nearly means correspond.

21. (B) The author states that with financial stability, people can afford to buy more meat, which implies that along with financial success comes a more robust daily diet.

22. (C) In lines 27–28, the author states that "methane's global warming potential is 25 times worse" than that of carbon dioxide.

23. (D) In this context, the word "potential" most nearly means capability.

24. (B) The only statement that can be inferred from Passage 1 is that until recently, the role of older fathers in health problems was not public knowledge. The first sentence of the second paragraph states that the issue "is not commonly known."

25. (D) Both passages discuss possible causes of health problems during pregnancy.

26. (A) In this context, the word "presents" most nearly means exhibits.

27. (C) The main point of Passage 2 is that the physical development of the brain during pregnancy can affect mental health. The only answer choice that supports this premise suggests that disorders may be triggered when the nerves that pull the cortex into place are damaged during fetal development.

28. (D) Chromosomal abnormalities are problems in the formation of chromosomes.

29. (D) The assertion is that the most well-known complication of advanced maternal age is chromosomal abnormality. The answer choice that undermines this is the one that states that only 13 percent of people polled knew that Down syndrome is a health complication from pregnancy in women over 40.

30. (A) The author of Passage 2 likens the shape of intestines to that of the cerebral cortex, thereby illustrating the meandering nature of the brain's structure.

31. (A) In this context, the word "irregularities" most nearly means deviations.

32. (D) Passage 1 is concerned with genetics, while Passage 2 is concerned with physical development at the fetal stage.

33. (C) In this context, the word "fundamental" most nearly means essential.

34. (A) Based on the statement that other public schools are restricted by "quotas that hamper success," the author would most likely describe nonchartered public schools as ineffective.

35. (E) In this context, the word "adhere" most nearly means obey.

36. (C) In the second paragraph, the author implies that state laws restrict progress and achievement.

37. (B) It can be inferred that the author believes that academic results are equal to success, based on the statement in the last paragraph that charter schools "are held accountable for academic results rather than the quotas that hamper success."

38. (E) The author's conclusion is that charter schools are more successful than other types of schools. Choice (E) provides information on the proportion of charter schools that have failed precisely due to the issues that the charter school concept was supposed to avoid, such as poor management and poorly performing students.

39. (A) The primary purpose of the passage is to promote an increase in the number of charter schools.

40. (B) In this context, the word "arid" most nearly means scorched.

41. (B) The main point of the passage is that, although desalination is currently expensive, it will grow in popularity as other means of getting fresh water become equally expensive. The only statement that supports this point is statement II.

42. (C) The harmful effects of desalination to the environment are not mentioned in the passage.

43. (B) In this context, the word "laudable" most nearly means praiseworthy.

44. (D) The author states that although steps to curb fresh water use in developed nations "are laudable, more needs to be done," which suggests that the author believes developed nations are still too careless with fresh water supplies.

45. (A) In this context, the word "adamant" most nearly means resolute.

46. (C) The phrase "with eyes like saucers" means that Nana was looking around in awe, with eyes wide open.

47. (E) The word "Quickly!" was repeated mainly to indicate the fear and urgency that Nana's mother felt as Nana smudged the chalk from her coat.

48. (D) The author uses the phrase "she was tough as old boots" to mean that Nana's mother was strong and brave.

49. (A) The narrator would likely describe Nana's story about wiping the chalk from her mama's coat as thrilling, as she was both enthralled and entertained, especially since she "laughed heartily" at the story's conclusion. The father would describe it as poignant (choice (B)) or emotional (choice (D)), since he was able to grasp the risk his mother and grandmother had taken that day.

50. (D) The word "mischievous," used to describe Nana's smile as she recollected her adventure, most nearly means playful.

51. (C) Nana says that "Da" had sent her mother letters and was waiting for them, with a job and a room to live in. Therefore, it can be inferred from the passage that Nana's father had gone to America ahead of them to find work.

52. (C) In this context, the word "interjected" most nearly means interrupted.

53. (A) The Sumer civilization was the first to practice full-scale agriculture.

54. (C) The author states that the people of the Sumer civilization created a surplus of storable food and therefore no longer had to migrate.

55. (B) Since the passage says, "We also cannot gather archaeological evidence of wine-making before the use of pottery as a storage vessel for wine," it can be inferred from Passage 2 that evidence of wine has only been conclusive when taken from hard, nonwooden vessels with porous surfaces.

56. (D) The authors of both passages discuss the early stages of full-scale agriculture.

57. (C) Passage 1 doesn't mention migration away from Mesopotamia.

58. (A) One of the differences between the two passages is that more is known about the Sumer civilization and less is known about when winemaking began. This makes answer choice (A) a strong one and choice (B) a poorer one, since Passage 2 is more speculative than Passage 1. Agriculture is discussed in both passages, thereby eliminating choice (C), while Passage 1 covers the advantages of permanent settlement more than Passage 2, thereby eliminating choice (D).

59. (E) In this context, the word "indisputable" most nearly means irrefutable.

60. (C) In the last paragraph of Passage 1, by stating that "the Sumer civilization deserves the title of 'cradle of civilization' for all of humanity," the author expresses admiration for the accomplishments of the Sumerians.

61. (E) The author mentions "current scientific methods" in Passage 2 in order to suggest that with more advanced technology, we may be able to prove wine's origins.

62. (A) The tone of Passage 1 is more laudatory than that of Passage 2, since the author of Passage 1 uses phrases such as "extraordinary civilization," "remarkable people," and "exceptional achievements."

63. (D) This answer choice merely elaborates on the importance of agriculture to the existence of human civilization. All of the other choices provide evidence that the title "cradle of civilization" can't be given to the Sumer civilization alone.

64. (B) According to Passage 2, "Experts believe that they discovered that fermented fruit beverages were safe to drink by accident." Therefore, winemaking began as a result of trial and error with early attempts at food storage.

65. (B) In this context, the word "exceptional" most nearly means incomparable.

66. (B) Based on the passage, the author would most likely describe the current energy crisis as a dangerous and urgent threat to global peace and economic stability.

67. (C) In this context, the word "nascent" most nearly means burgeoning.

68. (D) In the fourth paragraph, the author says that "in order to avoid dependence on hostile nations, the oil and gas industries in countries like Canada and the United States have turned to unconventional methods of extracting crude oil from less accessible areas," which suggests that political tensions are shaping the progress of the oil industry.

69. (E) This answer choice best describes the problem of food availability.

70. (D) In this context, the word "precipitously" most nearly means sharply.

71. (B) The sixth paragraph describes the problems surrounding the development of alternative sources of energy.

72. (B) In this context, the word "unconventional" most nearly means alternative.

73. (E) The idea that hydrofracking allows for the extraction of infinite deposits of crude oil is not stated anywhere in the passage.

74. (D) In this context, the word "dissemination" most nearly means distribution.

75. (A) The author states that unconventional methods of extracting crude oil, "while necessary, are nascent and controversial." Therefore, they represent new technologies that are essential, but experimental and divisive.

76. (B) In the last paragraph, the author states that the best way to deal with the situation is to design more fuel-efficient cars and provide more incentives for not using cars. Therefore, it would have to be true that other forms of energy consumption, such as electricity for homes and businesses, must not be a significant factor in the current energy crisis.

77. (C) The author states that "a nuclear meltdown would be unpredictable, deadly, and catastrophic." Therefore, the reason that some nations do not use nuclear power is that the effect of a plant meltdown would be too devastating.

78. (A) In this context, the word "catastrophic" most nearly means calamitous.

79. (C) The main point of the passage is that the role of women in society during the eighteenth and nineteenth centuries in Europe is a frequent subject in Austen's novels.

80. (D) Most of the heroines, like Austen herself, were educated but had little access to money. The fact that many of these women found themselves in similar situations is an example of a repeated theme, and the author of the passage provides examples of various Austen heroines in order to support the theory of recurring themes in Austen's novels.

81. (C) In this context, the word "inextricably" most nearly means thoroughly.

82. (D) The author would most likely describe the lives of women in the eighteenth and nineteenth centuries as precarious, since they had little control over basics like money or shelter.

83. (A) The only answer choice that is indicated in the passage is that even with an education, it was difficult for women to earn a living of their own.

84. (B) In this context, the word "recourse" most nearly means option.

85. (C) The main idea of Passage 1 is that a socioeconomic revitalization is taking place in the South Bronx.

86. (A) In this context, the word "dismal" most nearly means miserable.

87. (D) The passages address the same topic, which is the socioeconomic status of the South Bronx, but they arrive at different conclusions: where the author of Passage 1 sees revitalization, the author of Passage 2 does not.

88. (A) The author of Passage 2 displays a pessimistic attitude, since Passage 2 describes the problems that still exist in the South Bronx.

89. (E) In this context, the phrase "eke out" most nearly means to scrounge together.

90. (E) As noted in the answer to question No. 88, the tone of the second passage is pessimistic, since it mentions how many problems still trouble the South Bronx. This tone is consistent throughout; with the phrase "endless spiral of poverty," the author expresses a cynical assessment of the South Bronx's current economic standing.

91. (B) In this context, the word "considerable" most nearly means significant.

92. (A) The "house that Ruth built" was the original Yankees stadium where Babe Ruth played.

93. (D) In this context, the word "razed" most nearly means demolished.

94. (A) The authors of the two passages disagree on the topic of how much the quality of life in the South Bronx has improved since the 1970s.

95. (B) It can be inferred that both authors would agree that the South Bronx fell into deep disrepair in the late twentieth century.

96. (E) The only statement that can be inferred from the information in the passage is that men exposed to more testosterone in the womb are more likely to have greater control over their bodies.

97. (A) In this context, the word "advances" most nearly means improvements.

98. (B) Higher prenatal testosterone levels could have a greater influence on a person's physical characteristics than inherited genetic factors.

99. (B) The first paragraph states that we know more about the human fetus today because of expanded research in chemistry and advances in modern medicine.

100. (A) In this context, the word "execute" most nearly means perform.

Chapter 2: Set 2 Questions

101. (D) The conclusion of the passage is that the common law system's reliance entirely on prior decisions means its decisions can quickly grow outdated, and the legislative process is a slow and cumbersome way to change laws. Answer choice (D) speaks directly to this concern and provides evidence to the contrary.

102. (A) In this context, the word "precedent" most nearly means previous example.

103. (A) The last paragraph begins with the statement "Clearly, the civil law system is superior." The author backs up this statement with the observations that prior decisions can quickly become outdated and that changing them through legislative means is a poor, often time-consuming method. In summary, the author's attitude toward common law in the last paragraph indicates that the author sees common law as a stagnant, obsolete legal system.

104. (B) The Latin words *stare decisis* are a term for the guiding tenet of common law, as stated in lines 9–11.

105. (B) In this context, the word "cumbersome" most nearly means unwieldy.

106. (C) The author's main point is that honesty and trustworthiness is an essential element of online interaction. The statement that best supports this point is that the most useful and prolific sites provide dependable layers of security.

107. (E) In this context, the word "harnessed" most nearly means utilized.

108. (A) The phrase "the dark side" is symbolic of the destructive aspects of Internet use.

109. (A) The passage notes that websites "can be harnessed to benefit everyone"—the key words being "to benefit everyone"—in other words, to help society.

110. (D) In order to show how Web science covers both positive and negative aspects of the Web, the author discusses "the dark side of the Internet's capabilities" in the second paragraph. As examples of this dark side, "identity theft and cyberstalking" are cited; these illustrate the dangerous aspect of Web activity.

111. (C) The author uses "micro" and "macro" examples of Internet use to provide the scope of Web science's objectives. The smallest online exchanges between people and the interactions with a global effect are all relevant to Web science.

112. (B) In this context, the word "interactions" most nearly means exchanges.

113. (B) It can be inferred from the passage that the narrator is a horse. The first paragraph has several revealing details, such as those in lines 2–4.

114. (D) The narrator believes that "some new change must be at hand," because he is being specially groomed.

115. (C) The narrator describes Willie as "half anxious, half merry," meaning that Willie is nervous, but enthusiastic.

116. (C) The narrator is a horse, and the "chaise" is a vehicle in which two people can ride, since Willie gets in alongside his grandfather. The third paragraph mentions a journey of a mile or two, implying that Willie and his grandfather have been transported via the chaise. Based on this context, a chaise is a type of horse-drawn carriage.

117. (D) In this context, the word "shrubbery" most nearly means bushes.

118. (A) Mr. Thoroughgood is offering Black Beauty to the sisters "on trial," meaning that they can "try him out" and observe whether he is a good fit without obligation.

119. (B) In this context, the word "stately" most nearly means dignified.

120. (E) When the stately lady makes this remark to Mr. Thoroughgood, she means that his advice, or "recommendation," is valuable to her.

121. (B) In this context, the word "objection" most nearly means protestation.

122. (C) The description of the tall lady suggests that she is frail. She is described as pale, and because she is leaning on a "much younger lady," she may also be advanced in years.

123. (B) When the narrator says he was "placed in a comfortable stable," he means that he was left in a well-kept barn.

124. (B) It can be inferred that when the narrator says that Joe, the groom, "almost started," he means that Joe was greatly surprised. "To start" can mean to jump back in surprise.

125. (C) The narrator says that "for now he was a fine-grown young fellow, with black whiskers and a man's voice." It can therefore be inferred that the narrator doesn't remember Joe Green, because Joe has grown up since the narrator last saw him.

126. (C) The narrator says that he has a scar on his neck from where he was bled, which Joe discovers. When Joe says that the narrator was "badly served out," he means that the narrator was mistreated.

127. (C) The author states that if the moon had always faced the same way, it would have more craters on one side; therefore, something must have spun the moon 180 degrees to its current orientation. It can be inferred from this statement that there aren't disproportionately more craters on one side of the moon.

128. (B) In this context, the word "coalesced" most nearly means combined.

129. (A) The author states, "There have been a number of hypotheses on how it came to exist, but the most widely accepted explanation . . .". Therefore, the author suggests that other explanations for the moon's existence have been deemed unlikely.

130. (D) The author says that "an impact occurred between Earth and another object that was likely as big as Mars, which forced tons of material into orbit." Therefore, the author implies that the collision between Earth and the other object was colossal.

131. (A) The author suggests the possibility that "a collision with a large asteroid" spun the moon 180 degrees to its current orientation.

132. (C) In this context, the word "orientation" most nearly means position.

133. (E) The statistic, that nearly one in 200 people has a peanut allergy, is a high ratio. The author therefore uses it to illustrate how common peanut allergies are in the United States.

134. (B) The author's conclusion is that no-tolerance policies are the "only effective approach to protecting children who are allergic from suffering a fatal reaction." However, other methods, such as having epinephrine injectors in schools and alerting teachers about which children are afflicted, keep incidents of reactions low.

135. (C) In this context, the word "avert" most nearly means avoid.

136. (D) According to the passage, "children with this allergy are often at serious risk when eating foods outside the home, away from the watchful eyes of their parents and guardians." Therefore, children are most at risk when eating out, because they are not being supervised by an adult who is familiar with their allergy.

137. (A) The sentence before the "no tolerance" statement talks about the risk people with peanut allergies face, while the sentence after the statement notes that a no-tolerance policy is the "only effective approach." With the seriousness of the allergy thus explained, answer choice (A) is the most logical.

138. (B) The author's conclusion is that Quechua would have been the most common language spoken in South America if the Spanish hadn't ended the Inca Empire's dominance. This is weakened by the statement that the Inca Empire was already on the brink of collapse when the Spanish arrived.

139. (A) In this context, the word "extensive" most nearly means widespread.

140. (C) According to the passage, the Inca Empire was extensive, since it "stretched along nearly the entire western coast of the South American continent."

141. (B) In this context, the word "subjugation" most nearly means suppression.

142. (A) Since the Incas used Quechua to "ease communications across the empire," it can be inferred that *lingua franca* means a language used to make communication possible between people who don't share a language.

143. (D) The conclusion states that lawsuits "made Napster a worldwide phenomenon." The author therefore assumes that Napster was a relatively unknown service before lawsuits were reported in the news.

144. (C) In this context, the word "circumventing" most nearly means avoiding.

145. (A) In lines 4–5, the author states that Napster "allowed people to exchange files between computers, thereby circumventing the need to go to a store and purchase an album or single recording." It can be inferred from this statement that the music being shared was in a digital format.

146. (A) The author states that "despite the efforts of companies, artists, and governments, new file-sharing programs appear every day." The author would therefore likely agree that file-sharing programs are prolific, despite efforts to stop illegal downloads.

147. (D) The author states that Napster debuted in June 1999 and that the creator was being sued just six months later. These dates reveal how quickly the RIAA moved to sue Napster.

148. (A) In this context, the word "specter" most nearly means presence.

149. (A) After its introductory paragraph, Passage 1 puts forward three different points of view. The first expresses the viewpoint of proponents of plus-size models, the second expresses the viewpoint of their detractors, and the third expresses a third viewpoint. Answer choice (A) is correct, since it states that the author's primary purpose in writing Passage 1 is to discuss opinions about plus-size fashion.

150. (C) The authors of the two passages would most likely disagree on whether the industry is responsible for how it markets products and images to society. The author of Passage 1 would say that the industry is responsible, while the author of Passage 2 would say that it is a matter of personal responsibility.

151. (A) In this context, the word "bombard" most nearly means overwhelm.

152. (D) The author's attitude toward plus-size marketing in Passage 1 can best be described as antagonistic. The author says that it "should not exist at all" (line 18) and that it is "tremendously damaging" (lines 20–21).

153. (B) In this context, the word "pernicious" most nearly means destructive.

154. (B) The author of Passage 1 says that the fashion industry "should only show images of people who are fit and trim" in marketing campaigns. The author would therefore most likely agree that the fashion industry should emphasize a trim, athletic figure as the ideal body type.

155. (B) In this context, the word "proactive" most nearly means energetic.

156. (D) Both passages mention the fact that the fashion industry has been accused of portraying women's bodies through the media in ways that are harmful and unreasonable.

157. (A) In this context, the word "misnomer" most nearly means an unsuitable term.

158. (A) The word "however" is often important in a passage, since it indicates that the author is about to pivot and make a point different from what has gone before. In this instance, the words immediately following "However" suggest that agencies and designers should not be blamed for the eating behaviors of their models or of adolescents in society, since "it is not up to the industry to edit its message."

159. (A) The only statement that can be directly inferred from the passage, especially the information provided in the first paragraph, is that progress is being made against all cancers, in particular the most common types.

160. (E) In this context, the word "diminishing" most nearly means shrinking.

161. (B) The passage, as well as the author's tone, supports the statement that regional differences in lung cancer trends underscore the success of tobacco control programs. California is given as an example of a state with a successful tobacco control program.

162. (D) California's highly successful program is mentioned in direct comparison with states where lung cancer death rates are on the rise.

163. (B) In this context, the word "pervasiveness" most nearly means ubiquity.

164. (A) The author focuses much of the passage on the relationship between smoking and incidences of lung cancer, and even states explicitly that lung cancer is "firmly influenced by behavior" (lines 25–26).

165. (A) The second paragraph mostly serves to explain why different states and regions have different lung cancer death rates.

166. (C) The primary purpose of the passage is to provide an update on trends in cancer incidence and death rates in the United States, as well as an in-depth analysis of smoking-related lung cancer.

167. (A) The authors of the report conclude that the decreases in incidence and death rates "must be seen as a starting point rather than a destination," implying that more work needs to be done. Therefore, efforts in prevention, early detection, and treatment should be regularly evaluated and improved.

168. (A) The only statement that is NOT supported in the passage is that it is important to reach underserved, low-income cancer patients in the communities where they live. The author doesn't explicitly discuss patients who may be overlooked or ignored because of their socioeconomic status.

169. (E) In this context, the word "implement" most nearly means apply.

170. (B) The third paragraph contains statements by the director of the North American Association of Central Cancer Registries. The author included this paragraph to underscore the facts presented in the second paragraph.

171. (A) Pollution from automobiles could be another example of the "environmental factors" mentioned.

172. (C) In this context, the word "augment" most nearly means advance.

173. (D) The only statement that the author would be likely to agree with, based on the information in the passage and the tone of the language used, is that hoarding is a debilitating behavioral condition.

174. (E) The passage concludes, "The mental health community has only recently begun an intensive study of hoarding." The statement that most supports this conclusion is that hoarding is a relatively new syndrome for the mental health community.

175. (A) In this context, the word "quotidian" most nearly means commonplace.

176. (C) The first paragraph mostly serves to introduce the problem of hoarding to the reader and describe its symptoms.

177. (E) In this context, the word "escalate" most nearly means intensify.

178. (D) It can be inferred that the Navajo language was successful, because few people in the world could understand it.

179. (A) The main point of Passage 2 is that although the Navajo soldiers are the most renowned, they were not the original codetalkers.

180. (E) The author mentions the admission by the Japanese chief of intelligence in order to emphasize just how successful the use of Navajo was as a code.

181. (C) In this context, the word "hunch" most nearly means intuition.

182. (C) The topic introduced in Passage 1 is the use of Native American languages as military code, specifically the use of the Navajo language in World War II. Both passages discuss this issue. However, Passage 2 provides an alternative perspective by explaining that Choctaw was the first language to be so used and that Choctaw soldiers are not as famous as Navajo soldiers.

183. (D) In this context, the word "exploits" most nearly means courageous acts.

184. (B) These lines explain how "recent Hollywood movies and TV documentaries" have given renown to Navajo codetalkers in society today.

185. (C) The conclusion of Passage 1 is that the "the exploits of these heroic soldiers are finally making their way into mainstream American history." The author of Passage 2 would most likely respond by pointing out that this is only true for the Navajo soldiers and that Choctaw soldiers still do not receive the same recognition.

186. (B) In this context, the word "fanfare" most nearly means celebration.

187. (A) The author of Passage 2 says that the officer's "hunch proved to be correct." The hunch was that Choctaw could be used as "an unbreakable code that the U.S. Army could use to get information past the Germans." We can therefore infer that although Choctaw was used openly, it was never deciphered by the Germans.

188. (C) It can be inferred that both authors would agree that the U.S. military owes many victories to the Native American codetalkers.

189. (E) Because the author of Passage 1 points out that Navajo codetalking won many battles and that the Navajo code was never broken or deciphered, the author would most likely agree with the statement that Navajo was the most successful military code in modern history.

190. (C) In this context, the word "company" refers to a military unit.

191. (B) "The Red Planet" is used as a metaphor for Mars because of its red surface. In the second paragraph, the authors mentions "dark patches on its red surface."

192. (C) The author's attitude toward Mars observation is very positive; it can therefore be best described as enthusiastic.

193. (D) The passage notes the earliest recorded observations of Mars, goes on to discuss early telescopic images, and then considers modern efforts to view the planet and its surface. It can be assumed, therefore, that the author's primary purpose in writing the passage is to describe the history of Mars observation.

194. (A) Based on the information provided in the passage's conclusion, the author would most likely agree that this millennium has ushered in a new chapter in Mars observation.

195. (B) An "unmanned spacecraft" is a programmable machine that humans can control. Therefore, the phrase is analogous to a robot.

196. (D) In this context, the word "uncharted" most nearly means unexplored.

197. (A) In this context, the word "inflicted" most nearly means imposed.

198. (A) The answer can be found at the end of the first paragraph. After noting that the Tower of London was first used as a residence, the passage states that it "became a symbol of the power and oppression inflicted upon the citizens of Great Britain by these new rulers." Answer choice (A) conveys this idea best.

199. (E) In this context, the word "infamous" most nearly means notorious.

200. (E) The author mentions the rarity of executions at the Tower in order to emphasize that "despite its infamous reputation," this negative perception of the Tower is unfounded.

Chapter 3: Set 3 Questions

201. (A) The only answer choice that can be inferred from the content of the passage is that both commercial and wild bees are affected by CCD.

202. (C) The author of the passage does not state that the pollination of luxury crops keeps bees from pollinating wild plants.

203. (A) The author's conclusion is that more research needs to be done to find the actual causes of CCD in order to prevent the loss of wild plants and nutritious staple crops. Answer choice (A) argues that lack of research isn't the problem; it's a lack of cooperation from federal and state governments.

204. (D) The only answer choice that can be inferred from the first paragraph is that the causes of CCD are complex. The author states, "Recent studies have revealed that there is likely more than one factor affecting the bees, rather than a single cause."

205. (B) The "symbiotic relationship" of bees and plants is mutually beneficial. The bees seek food and pollinate the plants at the same time. This is analogous to cleaner shrimp that feed off the bacteria living on bigger fish that would otherwise make the bigger fish sick.

206. (C) The only statement not supported by the passage is that many companies refuse to hire workers younger than 18.

207. (D) In this context, the word "ineptitude" most nearly means incompetence.

208. (C) The first sentence states that "there are several forms of age-related bias" and gives examples of two forms of ageism.

209. (B) In this context, the word "manifests" most nearly means reveals.

210. (A) The author uses words such as "insidious" and "perpetrated." Therefore, the author's attitude toward ageism can best be described as appalled.

211. (D) The author's primary purpose in writing Passage 1 is to describe the history of female soldiers in the Civil War.

212. (A) In this context, the word "unconventional" most nearly means unusual.

213. (B) The only statement that the author of Passage 2 would agree with is that the existence of soldier-women was no secret during or after the Civil War.

214. (A) The author of Passage 2 mentions Mary Owens in order to provide evidence of eyewitness accounts and published reports.

215. (D) In this context, the word "fascination" most nearly means interest.

216. (A) The authors of both passages discuss women who fought in the Union and Confederate armies.

217. (D) In these lines, the author of Passage 1 suggests reasons why women were able to successfully pass as men in the camps.

218. (A) The attitude of the author of Passage 1 toward women who fought in the Civil War can best be described as reverent.

219. (B) The author implies that specific details of these women's experiences were often not included in published accounts.

220. (E) In this context, the word "embedded" most nearly means rooted.

221. (D) Both passages address the issue of women who fought in the Union and Confederate armies. Passage 1 is simply an historical account of their existence, while Passage 2 describes how well known they were during and after the Civil War.

222. (A) The "rank and file" refers to the ordinary soldiers of an army, excluding the officers, who lived in the camps.

223. (B) In this context, the word "unscathed" most nearly means unharmed.

224. (B) The conclusion is that building owners and city officials need to provide more incentives to get people to stop driving to city centers. The statement that best supports this conclusion is that people are less willing to drive into the city if they have to pay a lot for parking.

225. (A) In this context, the word "congestion" most nearly means overcrowding.

226. (E) The first sentence of the passage defines urban planning. This is followed by expansion of the topic, including factors that affect urban planners as well as possible activities of urban planners.

227. (E) According to these lines, one aspect of an urban planner's job is to focus on "the patterns that emerge out of daily life." Therefore, an urban planner would need to research and analyze metropolitan routines.

228. (D) According to the passage, parking space requirements have changed since the 1950s, since minimal free parking is supposed to prevent people from driving downtown.

229. (A) In this context, the word "purview" most nearly means scope of responsibility.

230. (B) The narrator of the passage is none of the people mentioned in the other choices; therefore, the narrator is a third-party observer.

231. (E) In this context, the word "interminable" most nearly means endless.

232. (A) In the first paragraph, the narrator describes the snow falling on Paris "with rigorous, relentless persistence," but then states that "sometimes there was a lull."

233. (B) The narrator goes to great lengths to describe the snowfall as heavy and seemingly unending. While not overtly asserting that the cold would be uncomfortable, the author does state that the patrol went by "beating their hands," implying that it was very cold and that a person would probably not enjoy being out in such weather.

234. (B) In this context, the word "propounded" most nearly means suggested.

235. (A) Villon is described as an "irreverent dog," because his "alternative" theories on the snow were sinful and impious speculation.

236. (E) In this context, the phrase "raw and pointed" is used to indicate that the air outside was bitterly cold.

237. (C) In this context, the word "grotesque" most nearly means hideous.

238. (D) The falling snow is a key descriptive element of this passage, and this includes the cathedral itself, with references to snow in niches and on statues and gargoyles.

239. (D) In this context, the word "decently" most nearly means abundantly.

240. (A) Based on this context, the word "burghers" most nearly means citizens of a town.

241. (B) The tone of the passage can best be described as ominous.

242. (B) The time is not explicitly mentioned, but a patrol would typically be out at night; furthermore, it is stated that "burghers were long ago in bed." The lamp in the church reinforces the lateness of the hour.

243. (E) The purpose of the last paragraph is to imply that the people inside were devising a wicked plan.

244. (C) The half-obliterated footprints were the result of Villon and his friends having been inside the house for a while. Their original footprints would be covered with fresh snow.

245. (D) At no time does the narrator say anything about Villon and his friends becoming priests; they were merely in the company of an old priest.

246. (A) In this context, the word "alien" most nearly means unknown.

247. (E) The narrator mentions Porter's educational background as a student of art and architecture to help explain why his drawings were so exceptional.

248. (D) The author uses words like "impressive" and "beautifully detailed" to describe Porter's work. Therefore, the word that best describes the author's attitude toward Porter is admiration.

249. (D) The main point of the passage is that Porter was both a gifted artist and fearless explorer.

250. (C) The only statement that can be inferred from the last paragraph is that Porter's sketches and paintings can be appreciated on many levels—for example, as works of art and as scientific documents.

251. (B) The author uses the expression "filled the cave with thunder" to mean that Shere Khan roared loudly.

252. (B) Shere Khan had barged into Father Wolf's home, making Father Wolf angry, but Father Wolf was still deferential to Shere Khan. This implies that Shere Khan was highly respected and feared.

253. (E) The descriptions of Mother Wolf imply that she was a brave, fearsome fighter. Her nickname was "The Demon," and even Shere Khan knew he would be no match for her that night.

254. (C) At no time does the narrator suggest that Shere Khan left because the cubs would be in danger during the fight.

255. (A) In this context, the word "gravely" most nearly means solemnly.

256. (C) The only statement that can be inferred from Passage 1 is that the Marine Corps played a very large role in the military conflicts of the twentieth century.

257. (A) The author's primary purpose in writing Passage 2 is to describe the history of Puerto Ricans serving in the U.S. military.

258. (B) The "something" mentioned is that the Marines were able to deploy "at a moment's notice."

259. (D) Passage 1 and Passage 2 discuss the same topics, but they focus on different aspects of the topics. Both address the Spanish-American War, the addition of new U.S. territories—particularly, Puerto Rico—and the Marine Corps.

260. (C) The author uses many positive words and laudatory language while discussing Puerto Ricans in the U.S. military. Therefore, the author's attitude in Passage 2 can best be described as complimentary.

261. (A) The author of Passage 1 would most likely agree with the statement that the explosion of the USS *Maine* led Congress to declare war on Spain in 1898.

262. (C) Since the Marine Corps is the main topic of Passage 1, answer choices (A), (B), and (E) can be eliminated. The passage does not discuss growing pains or early problems encountered by the Marines, so choice (D) can be eliminated.

263. (E) Both authors would agree that the Marines would play a vital role in future conflicts both in the Pacific Ocean and in Europe.

264. (D) In this context, the word "sovereignty" most nearly means control.

265. (B) In this context, "ultimate sacrifice" is symbolic of giving your life for your country.

266. (D) The main point, that the jail population of the United States has grown to an "alarming size," is best supported by the fact that there are more people in jail today than there were 20 years ago.

267. (B) In this context, the word "efficacy" most nearly means competence.

268. (A) In the third paragraph, the information that the author provides suggests that the increase of incarceration in America is felt most strongly by minorities.

269. (C) The first paragraph serves mostly to explain the current state of U.S. corrections procedures.

270. (C) Although the first part of the passage lauds the decrease in crime in America, this is balanced in the passage by noting the increased prison population. The passage states that the jailed population is at an "alarming size," and one factor is that people are serving longer sentences.

271. (A) It can be inferred from the passage that trichromats can detect more colors than dichromats.

272. (A) The author suggests that fish, birds, and humans eventually went down different evolutionary paths.

273. (E) The only statements that can be inferred from the passage are statements II and III. The passage doesn't state how many different colors dichromats can see. The passage does state that dichromacy is predominant in human males, which means some females are dichromats, and that dichromats can see only blue and green pigments.

274. (C) The statement that would most undermine the author's conclusion about the role of ripe fruit in trichromacy is the one that gives an alternative theory. Answer choice (C) states that the ability to detect skin flushing, and thereby mood, may have influenced trichromatic vision.

275. (E) In this context, the word "distinguish" most nearly means to differentiate.

276. (D) The conclusion that "employers today should not overlook the option of tele-commuting" is best supported by all of the statements except answer choice (D), which implies that workers who begin as telecommuters may eventually leave the company, since they prefer self-employment.

277. (C) The main idea of the passage is that telecommuting is beneficial, and the second paragraph lists some of its advantages. Both virtual offices (answer choice (A)) and electricity and rental costs (choice (B)) are aspects of telecommuting, but not the main point of the second paragraph, so they can be eliminated. The paragraph mentions globalization (choice (D)) and living far from urban centers (choice (E)), but not as benefits of telecommuting.

278. (B) The author believes that telecommuting is a positive move forward for employers, so the author's attitude toward telecommuting can be described as enthusiastic.

279. (E) The main idea of the passage is that telecommuting is beneficial. Only answer choice (E) supports this idea.

280. (A) Based on the author's warnings in lines 17–19, the author would most likely agree with the statement that companies considering telecommuting should check on legal issues, union rules, and zoning laws.

281. (A) In this context, the word "facile" most nearly means easy.

282. (D) The passage does not support the statement that the Portuguese were the last Europeans to enter the spice trade.

283. (C) The key phrase in the passage refers to the Portuguese as "knowledgeable operators of new maritime equipment." This supports the statement that the Portuguese used recent developments in maritime technology to their advantage.

284. (D) The passage refers to the Portuguese as "skilled mapmakers." Bartolomeu Dias, Vasco da Gama, and the Cape of Good Hope are mentioned in the passage, but the statements in answer choices (A) and (B) are not supported by the passage. Likewise, choice (C) is unsupported. The statement in choice (E) that "all other destinations were easy to find" is rather extreme—a clue to its being incorrect.

285. (E) The last sentence of the passage notes how other European countries became eager to acquire territories overseas, and as a result of this increased competition, "the Portuguese Empire began its slow but steady decline."

286. (B) The narrator uses the phrase "ripe but well-cared-for" to describe the ladies at lunch.

287. (E) In this context, the word "parapet" most nearly means wall.

288. (C) The narrator's description of the people, with their "guidebooks and fumbling for tips," suggests that they are tourists.

289. (A) The narrator says, "The luncheon hour was long past," but it is not yet dinnertime, so the scene must take place in the late afternoon.

290. (B) In this context, the word "extremity" most nearly means edge.

291. (D) The conversation in these lines serves mostly to give details about the relationship between Mrs. Slade and Mrs. Ansley.

292. (E) In dealing with the headwaiter, Mrs. Slade takes the lead, talking with him and paying him a tip. In contrast, Mrs. Ansley merely notes that the headwaiter was looking their way. It can thus be inferred that Mrs. Slade is more gregarious and confident than Mrs. Ansley.

293. (A) The term "retrospective" suggests viewing the past. This is reinforced by Mrs. Slade's remark that follows: "It's a view we've both been familiar with for a good many years."

294. (A) The word "opulent" refers to wealth. This is reinforced by the facts that the two ladies are having lunch in Rome like they have many times in the past, they are able to tell the headwaiter just what they want and get it, and their two daughters are flying around the country to have tea. All of these clues point toward having wealth.

295. (C) After handing the headwaiter money (the "gratuity"), the headwaiter agrees that it is no problem for them to stay. In effect, the money has bought them the right to stay.

296. (B) The narrator uses the word "interpolated," which means interjected or interrupted. Mrs. Slade did not seem upset by the interruption, so answer choice (C) can be eliminated.

297. (C) In this context, the word "retreated" most nearly means withdrew.

298. (D) Answer choices (A), (B), and (C) are unsupported by the passage. The two women have been discussing the distant past, not the time since lunch (choice (E)).

299. (E) The passage contains the statement "Moonlight—moonlight! What a part it still plays in the lives of young lovers."

300. (A) In this context, the word "sentimental" most nearly means maudlin.

Chapter 4: Set 4 Questions

301. (A) Answer choice (B) is off topic. Choice (C) contains the word "only," which signals an extreme statement that is unlikely to be correct. Choices (D) and (E) are unsupported by the passage.

302. (B) It can be inferred that the brand name "the Met" eventually fell out of use.

303. (E) The author mentions the changes in order to imply that the owners of the Met made improvements as technology improved.

304. (E) The first two sentences of the second paragraph indicate that the railway made it easier to move around the city and led to increased settlement in the city's suburbs.

305. (D) In this context, the word "incorporated" most nearly means integrated.

306. (A) The passage explains in detail how *Pinguicula moranensis* captures and digests insects.

307. (B) In this context, "arthropods" is another word for insects.

308. (C) The author says that "Vegetation like *Pinguicula moranensis* is known to digest insects, because the soil on which they grow is devoid of the nutrients they require to thrive," so the insects provide nutrients that the soil cannot.

309. (E) The author is enthusiastic and appreciative of *Pinguicula moranensis*, so the author's tone can best be described as passionate.

310. (D) The author does not discuss how other insectivorous plants digest insects.

311. (B) The purpose of the first paragraph is to describe in detail the type of world that Belle Morgan stepped into.

312. (B) In this context, the word "supercilious" most nearly means pompous.

313. (A) The first paragraph describes at length the town as stately, proper, and "aristocratic." The fact that the town is located in New England is another clue, as is the reference to the war for independence.

314. (E) In this context, the word "decorous" most nearly means well-behaved.

315. (A) The term "ennui" means boredom. Lennox takes to looking out a window just to catch a passing glimpse of a stranger who seems lively; this is the behavior of a person who is immensely bored.

316. (D) The name Belle appears only at the end of the passage, but she is definitely the girl in the scarlet stockings. Kate, not Belle, is Lennox's sister, so answer choice (A) can be eliminated. Answer choices (B), (C), and (E) are unsupported by the passage.

317. (B) In this context, the word "irradicable" most nearly means entrenched.

318. (E) According to the passage, Belle cannot be described as meager.

319. (D) The author says that Belle "seemed to wake up the whole street, and leave a streak of sunshine behind it" and "the primmest faces relaxed into smiles," so she enchanted and delighted everyone she passed.

320. (B) In this context, the word "elastic" most nearly means flexible.

321. (D) The author says that Belle's presence is like "a whiff of fresh spring air [that] had blown through the street in spite of the December snow," making her a complete contrast to her surroundings.

322. (D) The narrator describes Belle as walking briskly to an unknown destination and that her hands and pockets were full of packages. The narrator never says that Belle is a nurse.

323. (C) Lennox is described as "lounging in the bay-window at about three PM, and watching the gray and scarlet figure pass" and that he "quite depended on the daily stirring-up."

324. (C) It can be inferred from the last paragraph that Lennox was usually the heart-breaker; the narrator states, "For the first time in his life, the 'Crusher' . . . got crushed."

325. (D) In this context, the word "affectations" most nearly means mannerisms.

326. (A) Answer choice (B) appears only in Passage 2, and choices (C) and (E) appear only in Passage 1. Passage 1 contains multiple references to Egypt, but not to its pyramids, so choice (D) can be eliminated.

327. (A) In this context, the word "commandeered" most nearly means seized.

328. (E) The author of Passage 2 is upset that the "shameful ownership of ill-gotten antiquities has continued unabated" and takes issue with nations that have "pilfered" antiquities from other countries.

329. (C) The author of Passage 1 states, "In the 2000s alone, 12 million items were given to the British Museum's Egyptian collections by benefactors from around the world." Therefore, millions of objects have been donated to the museum's Egyptian collections.

330. **(B)** The changes mentioned were to antiquities laws in Egypt to prohibit foreigners from funding and conducting excavations.

331. **(D)** As noted in the answer to question No. 328, the author of Passage 2 is outraged, making answer choices (C) and (D) possible candidates, since they use the words "protest" and "criticize." Since the author has a somewhat positive view of the United Nations due to its efforts to prohibit the illegal transfer of cultural artifacts, choice (C) can be eliminated.

332. **(A)** It is not true that the British Museum's Egyptian collections have been sequestered by the Egyptian government.

333. **(C)** The second paragraph of Passage 2 does not state that the UNESCO convention became U.S. law through the Convention on Cultural Property Implementation Act.

334. **(A)** The two passages are in direct opposition to each other.

335. **(D)** In this context, the word "pilfered" most nearly means stolen.

336. **(E)** It can be inferred from Passage 1 that the Egyptian galleries can display only a minuscule percentage of the British Museum's Egyptian holdings.

337. **(C)** In this context, the word "unabated" most nearly means unhindered.

338. **(B)** In this context, the word "sensibility" most nearly means consciousness.

339. **(E)** It is unclear why Marner lost consciousness, so answer choices (A) and (D) can be eliminated. There is no mention of a coma or fainting spells, so choices (B) and (C) can also be eliminated.

340. **(A)** Marner sees the color gold and reaches for it, believing it to be gold—in the form of coins—that he has somehow lost. Instead, he encounters a "sleeping child" with golden curls for hair.

341. **(B)** In this context, the word "agitated" most nearly means disconcerted.

342. **(C)** According to these lines, Marner at first assumed that he was dreaming of his sister, who had died when they were children.

343. **(E)** According to these lines, "the flame did not disperse the vision," meaning that Marner had expected the child to disappear.

344. **(D)** The last paragraph describes how the presence of the child awakens old, yet fond, recollections of Marner's own childhood.

345. **(B)** In these lines, the narrator says that "the thoughts were strange to him now, like old friendships impossible to revive," so Marner's sudden rush of memories were like long-ago friendships that seem lost forever.

346. (A) It can be inferred that the child had replaced Marner's lost gold and was his life's new treasure.

347. (A) The first sentence of the passage says that *La bohème* has an Italian libretto.

348. (D) A "collection of vignettes" is an anthology of stories.

349. (E) The author states that "the opera became an immediate international phenomenon," which implies that the opera has been performed in countries around the world.

350. (A) The author would most likely agree that the opera has an enduring likability and will be loved, in various forms, by many generations.

Chapter 5: Set 1: Low-Difficulty Questions

351. (A) The correct answer will contradict Angela's assumption that the job would be an "exciting adventure." *Prosaic* means boring, plain, and lacking liveliness.

352. (D) *Assiduous* means hardworking and diligent—exactly the type of student described.

353. (B) Her sister's being able to babysit was a lucky event for Janie, making *fortuitous* the correct answer.

354. (C) The insult was attributed, or *imputed*, to Shannon, but it was not her fault. Therefore, a *reconciliation*—an agreement after a quarrel—could occur.

355. (D) A part-time job at a deli probably would not pay much, making the salary *meager*, or small. The artist would therefore have to be *frugal* with her money, that is, thrifty and economical.

356. (E) The correct answer will mean the opposite of "original," since "dull" is the opposite of "exhilarating." *Hackneyed* means clichéd or worn out by overuse.

357. (C) Since the old man raised his voice angrily over what a child had done accidentally, he could be described as *rancorous*, that is, bitter or hateful.

358. (A) The saleswoman was probably becoming more and more *exasperated*—irritated or frustrated—as she was trying unsuccessfully to make the customer happy.

359. (C) By talking about his family and upbringing instead of his economic policies, the politician was *digressing*, or straying from the main point.

360. (A) Since the problem is described as "complicated" and the solution as "helpful," the only answer choice that makes sense is *sagacious*, which means wise.

361. (E) *Vindicated* means avenged or freed from allegation.

362. **(D)** Derek wishes to copy the lifestyle of Emily's family, which is described as "wealthy and fashionable." The only answer choice that makes sense in this context is *emulate*, which means to imitate, and *opulent*, which means rich and lavish.

363. **(A)** The correct answer choice will convey the opposite of "nervousness." *Nonchalant* means calm, casual, or seemingly unexcited.

364. **(E)** The speaker is recommending a calm and discreet approach, making *prudent* the correct answer choice.

365. **(B)** The only answer choice that is consistent with the phrase "overwrought and long-winded" is *florid*, which means extravagant or excessive.

366. **(E)** Since Carrie is described as "a huge asset," the correct answer choice will describe her positively. *Exemplary* means outstanding, and *diligent* means hardworking.

367. **(E)** The word "although" indicates that the correct answer choice will contradict "quite influential." The only choice that contradicts the phrase is *inconsequential*, which means unimportant or trivial.

368. **(D)** The statement describes a man deserving of respect because of his achievements, making *venerable* the correct answer choice.

369. **(B)** Since Truman disliked Stalin, the first word will be a negative one. However, the fact that Russia was also an ally means that the two men were on the same team. Therefore, the only appropriate word combination is *wary of*, which means suspicious of, and *collaborate*, which means to work together.

370. **(C)** Brenda hoped that her success would be permanent, so the correct answer choice will mean the opposite. *Ephemeral* means short-lived or fleeting.

371. **(A)** The mayor is described as "dishonest," which means that she was likely trying to harm the reputation of, or *discredit*, her opponent with her ads. Since the damaging ads were printed in the newspaper, they were *libelous*, which means defamatory.

372. **(B)** The attributes of the CEO's career are described as positive and indicate that she has been around for a long time, which corresponds with answer choice (B), *longevity*.

373. **(D)** Rockefeller is described as concerned with minute details, so the correct answer choice is *meticulous*, which means very careful with facts and details.

374. **(B)** Since Marie overcame "incredible obstacles" to get to the audition, the correct answer choice is *tenacious*, which means determined and resolute.

375. **(E)** Since Romeo decided on a tragic course of action before finding out the facts of the situation, his decision was *impetuous*, or hasty and reckless.

376. (B) While the coworkers seemed to be at odds, they actually got along quite well. Therefore, *amicable*, which means friendly and agreeable, is the correct answer choice.

377. (C) The description of greenhouse gases as harmful denotes that they would have a *deleterious*, or destructive, effect. Since Mary and Sam did not agree on the issue, their discussion was *querulous*, or confrontational.

378. (E) Since the children were loud and rowdy at Arlington Cemetery, where they should have been quiet and respectful, they did not display the proper *reverence* for the location.

379. (E) The correct answer choice will be the opposite of "deep." *Superficial* means shallow.

380. (A) When people flee a nation or regime, they usually seek *asylum*, or refuge, in another country.

381. (A) Connor's behavior is described as "mean-spirited," which implies that he does not like the new boyfriend very much. Therefore, *disdain*, which means contempt or hatred, and *condescending*, which means snobbish or patronizing, are the correct answer choice.

382. (B) The politician probably did not want to discuss the photographs, because they presented him in a bad light, and the tabloids would only publish them to be *provocative*, or to provoke a negative response.

383. (B) The girl's appearance is described as "out of place" at the concert. The only answer choice that fits the context is *anachronistic*, which means old-fashioned or obsolete.

384. (C) The police needed to be called because of the fights that resulted when the fans of the rival teams *converged*, or came together in the same place.

385. (C) Andrew's behavior is described as including "late-night parties and wild spending sprees," so *hedonistic*, which means wild and self-indulgent, is the correct answer choice.

386. (B) Sara's coach wanted her to hold back from obvious celebration after winning the game, making *suppress* and *jubilation* the correct answer choice.

387. (A) *Prosperity* means wealth or success, which correlates with the context of the politician's speech about education and creating jobs.

388. (B) Since the speaker needs to sneak into the house undetected, *surreptitiously*, which means secretly or covertly, is the best answer choice.

389. (D) The correct answer will reflect the fact that John has not been working at his new job very long and doesn't have much experience. A *novice* is a beginner.

390. (A) The speaker's *procrastination*, or putting off a task until the last minute, resulted in him failing the test, which was the *inevitable*, or expected, conclusion of his actions.

391. (E) The paint swatches were labeled "off-white" and "cream," which means the difference between them could be described as *subtle*, or nearly undetectable.

392. (D) The designer's talent was instinctive and untaught, which makes *intuitive* the best answer choice.

393. (C) Since the feelings of patriotism did not last very long, they could be described as *transient*, which means temporary or fleeting.

394. (D) The correct answer choice is *demagogue*, which means a leader or rabble-rouser who appeals to people's emotions or prejudices.

395. (B) *Perfidious*, which means disloyal or deceitful, describes people "who disagreed with" Henry VIII. *Usurp* means to seize or take over, which he did not allow anyone to do.

396. (E) Janelle is described as "insensitive" and "indiscreet," which are the opposite of *tactful*, which means careful and considerate.

397. (E) The Baroque period was noted for its "gold-leaf ornamentation and opulent use of color," so it was showy and flamboyant, making *ostentatious* the correct answer choice.

398. (A) The speaker needs to get rid of items that will not fit in his smaller apartment. These items are redundant and not needed, in other words, *superfluous*.

399. (A) The word "despite" indicates that Derek feels the opposite of "disagreeable." Therefore, *compassion*, meaning sympathy or kindness, is the correct answer choice.

400. (C) Since the congregation is described as "open and accepting," the man's hate speech was *incompatible*, or mismatched and unsuited, with their philosophy.

Chapter 6: Set 2: Medium-Difficulty Questions

401. (B) *Integrity* means uprightness of character and soundness of moral principle. Miranda was acting with integrity when she defended her classmate.

402. (E) Studious Cliff's influence is described as "good," which means that the first missing word will be positive. The nephew is described as "disrespectful," so the second word will be negative. The only answer choice that fits these criteria is *benevolent*, which means friendly and helpful, and *enervating*, which means tiresome and annoying.

403. (A) *Compromise*, which means to settle a dispute by terms agreeable to both sides, is the correct answer choice.

404. (C) The speaker would rather drive an outdated, simple car rather than a flashy new sports car. Therefore, the correct answer choice is *pretentious*, which means pretending to be important, intelligent, or cultured.

405. (E) Amundsen's achievements show him to be *intrepid*, meaning courageous and daring.

406. (A) The correct answer choice will convey the opposite of a scheduled life with careful planning. *Spontaneity* means impulsive action.

407. (E) The witnesses would not want other people to know that they had provided the police with information. Therefore, *anonymous*, which means nameless or without a disclosed identity, is the correct answer choice.

408. (B) The speaker wants Ellen to prove, or *substantiate*, her claim.

409. (A) The speaker describes the mother as having remarkable self-control, making *restrained*, which means calm and controlled, the correct answer choice.

410. (C) Being able to play a Mozart concerto at such a young age means that Madelyn was *precocious*, which means that she was unusually advanced or talented for her age.

411. (A) The detective needed to carefully review all the evidence, making *scrutinize* the correct answer choice.

412. (B) The speaker implies that what Katherine said about her is false. *Spurious* means fake, lacking authenticity, or not genuine.

413. (B) The ideas of the two people must be so far apart that they cannot agree, making *divergent*, which means conflicting or incompatible, the correct answer choice.

414. (C) The statement says that the church was "restored to its former glory." The correct answer choice is *renovation*, which means restoring a building to a good state of repair.

415. (E) The statement says that the circumstances would justify a late arrival. The correct answer choice is *extenuating*, which means reducing the seriousness of an offense by providing a good explanation.

416. (E) Another way of phrasing the statement is that Eric's not going to jail is *conditional*—that is, dependent—on a particular requirement. The requirement in this case is performing community service.

417. (A) The people in the statement were friends for decades, so the correct answer choice will describe a sense of friendship, or *camaraderie*.

418. (E) The speaker, in talking about the main characters in Shakespeare's play *Othello*, appears to be describing a conversation with the teacher about who the *antagonist*—that is, opponent or adversary—was.

419. (D) The first part of the statement says that Gwendolyn apologized to Stacy, that is, she acted *contrite*, which means sorry for something she had done. Gwendolyn only acted that way so that she would not receive *censure*—severe criticism or disapproval—from her friends, who said that she had done something wrong.

420. (D) Carol's allergy is potentially fatal, so she had to *abstain*—avoid—eating any treat that contained peanuts.

421. (D) The statement says that fame today is short-lived or transitory, making *evanescent* the correct answer choice.

422. (C) The evidence against the defense lawyer's client was damning, so the lawyer hoped that the jury would feel *empathy* toward his client, that is, that the jury would understand and share the defendant's feelings. Because of the jury's empathy, the lawyer hoped to obtain *leniency*—a sentence that was not severe—for his client.

423. (A) The clauses in this sentence describe opposites: the first clause describes a happy person, and the second describes someone who is disengaged from life, having been paralyzed and scarred as the result of an accident. The correct answer choice is *effervescent*, which means lively or energetic, and *reclusive*, which means solitary and alone.

424. (E) The scientist needed to work "around the clock" to find a cure, implying that the deadly bacteria spread quickly. *Virulent* means having a rapidly harmful effect.

425. (A) The statement is about a tour of the Grand Canyon in Arizona, where the landscape is *parched*, meaning hot and dry.

426. (B) The speaker is unable to focus on the explanation of the complex problem. This implies that the explanation is indirect and roundabout, making *circuitous* the correct answer choice.

427. (C) Based on the description of Eddie's Beatles collection, *reverence*, which means deep respect, accurately describes his feelings toward the band.

428. (B) Because the picture quality of the old films has diminished over time, the researchers are trying to find ways to improve, or *enhance*, them.

429. (E) The speaker is implying that the group is gathering to hear an entertaining account of the events of Uncle Clark's and Aunt Sue's trip, making *anecdotes* the correct answer choice.

430. (B) The second part of the statement implies that Carrie is going to need skill in deception, making *legerdemain*, which means sleight of hand, the correct answer choice.

431. (C) In the second part of the statement, the speaker is describing the essential element, or *linchpin*, of his or her argument.

432. (A) The statement says that the criminal frequently wore finely tailored suits, which implies that he had a *proclivity*—a particular tendency or inclination—for them.

433. (E) *Frivolous* means not sufficiently serious, useful, or sensible, which best describes the speaker's feelings about lawsuits by people seeking "money or fame."

434. (B) A *harangue* is loud, forceful speech intended to attack people or try to persuade them to do something, making it the correct answer choice.

435. (D) The terrible odor of the durian made Maria gag, and Terrence was not courteous enough to remove it before that happened. Therefore, the correct answer choice is *modicum*, which means a small amount, and *pungent*, which means sharp or strong.

436. (C) *Diaphanous* means light, fine, and almost transparent, which makes it the correct answer choice.

437. (A) The relationship between the brothers is *tenuous*, which means very weak.

438. (E) The correct answer choice will be the opposite of "laconic," which means using few words. *Garrulous* means excessively talkative, especially about trivial things.

439. (B) The statement is talking about the architecture of Paris, singling out "the beautiful bridges." The correct answer choice is *pulchritude*, which means beauty of form.

440. (A) The speaker felt that the politician was being insincere when talking about her family. The correct answer choice is *sanctimonious*, which means acting morally superior to others.

441. (D) The correct answer choice is *paragons*, which means models of excellence or perfection.

442. (B) The speaker was lying about experience in graphic design, since he or she has none. The correct answer choice is *mendacious*, which means lying or not telling the truth, and *neophyte*, which means a beginner.

443. (D) The missing word will mean to make fun of someone or something, making *deride* the correct answer choice.

444. (A) The correct answer choice is *implacable*, which means unforgiving and relentless.

445. (B) Sandra was obviously upset by the speaker's album choices. The correct answer choice is *vex*, which means to annoy or irritate.

446. (E) Karen's accusations would tarnish the speaker's reputation, making *defile* the correct answer choice.

447. (D) The correct answer choice will reflect the fact that Colin's career had hit rock bottom. *Nadir* means the lowest point.

448. (A) The statement describes a buffet that was full of a variety of dishes. *Replete* means well stocked or supplied.

449. (C) General McClellan is described as "unable to be decisive on the battlefield." The correct answer choice is *capricious*, which means fickle and unpredictable.

450. (B) A seminar is a meeting set up for the discussion of a topic. The correct answer choice is *repartee*, which means a conversation with spontaneous witty comments.

Chapter 7: Set 3: High-Difficulty Questions

451. (A) The statement says that Nancy was overwhelmed and implies that there was a large quantity of various materials, which means the correct answer choice is *surfeit*, which means an overabundant supply, and *multifarious*, which means diverse or various.

452. (B) Georgia states that Melissa "demands round-the-clock attention and constant compliments," meaning that the correct answer choice is *obsequious*, which means fawning and subservient.

453. (E) The correct answer choice is *juxtaposition*, which means placing two or more things side by side.

454. (C) The behavior that was recorded on tape and caused the CEO to be fired is described as "malicious," which means cruel. The correct answer choice is *invective*, which means insulting or abusive language.

455. (A) The new supervisor appears to be excessively concerned about following company rules, making *punctilious*, which means strict or fussy, the correct answer choice.

456. (D) The statement says that the man's coworkers found his jokes offensive, making *ribald*, which means crude or indecent, the correct answer choice.

457. (E) The statement presents two differing scenarios: while social media may seem like an innocuous, fun activity, its use can have disastrous consequences. The correct answer choice is *insidious*, which means subtly treacherous or harmful.

458. (C) The statement says that there are numerous job openings available to Carol, making *plethora*, which means an excess or overabundance, the correct answer choice.

459. (D) The correct answer choice is *fastidious*, which means meticulous and exacting. The aunt would be "the perfect proofreader," because she would discover problems in logic and errors in grammar.

460. (E) Since Melody is beautiful and enchanting, Chuck would want to speak with her as soon as possible. *Alacrity*, which means haste and eagerness, is the correct answer choice.

461. (B) Since the origin of the phrase is unknown, historians can only *surmise*, which means to guess or speculate, about where the phrase came from.

462. (C) The first missing word will be related in some way to "condescending," making *grandiloquence*—a pompous style of speech—and *cogent*—compelling or convincing—the correct answer choice.

463. (E) The consumerism is described as a negative element, leading to a "terrible chasm of debts." The correct answer choice is *pernicious*, which means highly injurious or destructive.

464. (D) The girls are trying to convince Nancy to join the Girl Scouts, so the correct answer choice is *cajole*, which means to persuade with flattery or gentle urging.

465. (A) The third word to describe Snow White will likely portray her as good and sweet, the opposite of the queen; *winsome* means charming and adorable. The second word will reflect the cruelty of the queen's decision to destroy Snow White; *nefarious* means flagrantly wicked or fiendish.

466. (B) Rebekah was "unable to make a choice"; *vacillate* means to waver or be indecisive.

467. (E) The statement says that the period is referred to as a war, because even though armies didn't fight physically, the threats and hostilities were just as dangerous. *Tantamount* means equal in value, significance, or effect.

468. (E) The local government's ideas are described as confusing. The correct answer choice is *obtuse*, which means difficult to understand.

469. (D) The statement says that the young man rejected his normal life to live in the wilderness. *Eschew* means to avoid or shun, especially on moral or practical grounds. *Conventional* means ordinary or commonplace.

470. (B) Jessica's guilt was revealed by her shuffling feet and shifty eyes. *Evince* means to show or be evidence of.

471. (D) The speaker cannot drive the carpool as promised, meaning he or she has to *rescind*—cancel or take back—the offer.

472. (A) *Somnolent*, which means drowsy or sleepy, is the correct answer choice.

473. (D) The governor's press conference was an attempt to prove that he was *contrite*, meaning repentant and eager to be forgiven.

474. (C) *Desecrate*, which means to violate the sacredness of a thing or place, is the correct answer choice.

475. (C) Since Emily had been doing well but her essay was full of "errors and obvious mistakes," the missing word will likely be negative. *Egregious* means conspicuously bad.

476. (E) The *hapless*, or unlucky, criminal was unable to escape, because the car he stole gave away his location.

477. (B) *Umbrage*, which means offense, is the correct answer choice.

478. (A) The aunt describes the youth as disrespectful, making *impertinent*, which means rude and insolent, the correct answer choice.

479. (E) Because the president's comments caused an increase in tensions between the two nations, the correct answer choice is *pejorative*, which means uncomplimentary or derogatory.

480. (B) *Extol* means to praise enthusiastically; the doctor would certainly praise the benefits of exercise and a good diet.

481. (C) The correct answer choice is *pallid*, which means pale and feeble, and *sanguine*, which means confident and optimistic.

482. (A) The speaker does not agree with the premise that the person cannot help the mother take out the trash, making *renounce*, which means to reject, the correct answer choice.

483. (D) Clara's brother teases her because her lifestyle changes were austere. The correct answer choice is *ascetic*, which means practicing restraint as a means of self-discipline, usually for religious reasons.

484. (A) *Tacit* means expressed without words, which aptly describes the refusal indicated by "the look on my mother's face."

485. (C) The statement warns against criticism of totalitarian regimes. *Decry* means to disapprove of openly. Answer choice (B), *rebuke*, has a similar meaning but is used to criticize only people.

486. (B) The correct answer choice will contrast with "energetic and funny" and will also imply that Harry is "shy or awkward." *Laconic* means using very few words.

487. (E) The crowds celebrating the end of World War II would be extremely joyful, making *jubilant* the correct answer choice.

488. (D) The correct answer choice is *fetid*, which means having a foul odor.

489. (C) The Boy Scouts were proud of themselves, but they were also happy to return to the comforts of home. *Concomitant* means accompanying, especially in a lesser or incidental way.

490. (C) Rupert's personality is described as caustic, which is a negative word, and the people in the statement try to avoid him. The correct answer choice is *mercurial*, which means characterized by rapid and unpredictable changes in mood, and *anathema*, which is someone or something intensely disliked or loathed.

491. (B) The socialite pouted and stomped her feet like a child throwing a tantrum. *Querulous*, which means petulant and whiny, is the correct answer choice.

492. (A) The young man was hardworking and persistent, making *pertinacious*, which means determined and persevering, the correct answer choice.

493. (A) The correct answer choice will contrast with "pleasant" and "kind-hearted." *Vitriolic* means harsh or caustic.

494. (B) The behavior of the defeated team was noble and generous, making *magnanimous* the correct answer choice.

495. (C) The politician describes the administration's foreign policy as "hostile" and says it will "lead to misunderstandings" and possibly to war. *Morass*, which means a quagmire or confusing situation, is the correct answer choice.

496. (D) Although Shannon was caught in the act of cheating, she defiantly denied that she had cheated. *Temerity*, which means audacity and impertinence, describes Shannon's attitude and is the correct answer choice.

497. (B) The correct answer choice will contrast with the main clause, which says that Apple accounts for only "five percent of sales." *Ubiquitous* means pervasive or widespread.

498. (B) The sounds produced by the stray cats were clearly unpleasant. *Cacophony*, which means harsh, discordant noise, is the correct answer choice.

499. (E) The speaker's change of plans was fortuitous; it was as if the speaker knew that the hurricane was coming. The correct answer choice is *prescient*, which means having knowledge of events before they happen.

500. (B) Being homecoming queen and class valedictorian was the culmination of Lauren's successes in her high school career, making *zenith* the correct answer choice.